Community Parades

Valuable Tips, Ideas and Procedures on
How to Plan, Organize, Produce, Run,
Stage or Start an
Outstanding Community Parade

Ed C. Tomlinson

Editor: Barbara Munson, Munson Communications
www.munsoncommunications.com

Cover design: Pam McKinnie, Concepts Unlimited
www.ConceptsUnlimitedInc.com

ISBN-13: 978-0692289440

ISBN-10: 0692289445

First edition

Printed in the United States of America

9 8 7 6 5 4 3 2 1

Diamond Publications
6655 West Jewell, #218
Lakewood, Colorado 80232.

Early praise for *Community Parades*...

"You have done a fantastic job covering all the numerous details that go into creating a topnotch parade. Anyone looking at starting a parade in their community or improving a current parade will definitely find tons of value in your book. It was very insightful to read. Thank you."

HaLee Walter

Parade Chair, Odessa, Washington. Population 910

♦♦♦

"Really impressed!"

Dave Miller

Executive Director, Burlington's Sound of Music Festival, www.soundofmusic.ca, *Canada's Largest Free Music Festival*

♦♦♦

"Community Parades by Ed C. Tomlinson is a much-needed, comprehensive compendium of practical tips for small- to mid-sized American parades. Written in a friendly, logical style, the book is an excellent resource that asks all the right questions and offers a wealth of answers gleaned from over a decade of hands-on experience—a must-read for any community-based American parade."

Charlotte J. DeWitt

International Events Limited, Boston, Massachusetts
Charlotte DeWitt, CFEE, (Certified Festival and Event Executive) has produced waterfront festivals and international events since 1979, working in some 29 countries throughout North America, Europe, "Down Under," Asia, and the Middle East.

DEDICATION

To My Wife Nancy

To the Tomlinson Family
Yesterday
Today
Tomorrow

ACKNOWLEDGMENTS

My appreciation extends to you the parade committees, who have helped make parades so much fun that they are true highlights of the year, both for the spectators and participants. There are 40,000-50,000 community parades each year. Most communities have a parade and some communities handle more. According to Wikipedia.org, there are 42,676 U.S. communities: 41,386 have populations under 25,000 so you are in good company. Leaving 1,290 communities with populations over 25,000. 19,289 are incorporated, and 23,387 unincorporated.

I'd also like to thank all those who instilled the parade fever in me over the years and lent me a hand. In particular, the 125 volunteers with the Arvada, Colorado Harvest Festival Parade, the 20,000 parade spectators, the 3,000 or so parade entry participants, the Arvada Jaycees, past and present, the dozens of city staff members and current and past council members of the City of Arvada. I'd also like to thank the Apex Parks and Recreation employees, all of whom helped to improve the parade.

Engaging with the Colorado and the IFEA, International Festivals and Events Association, experts was when I realized just how far a parade can improve. I'm like a kid in a candy store when I attend their conventions. These are the pros whose events often cost $250,000 to $3 million to put on. Their knowledge can help the tens of thousands of community parades across North America improve not only financially, but in spectator satisfaction, attendance, volunteers—in every aspect of producing a parade. IFEA's knowledge is readily available at the FREE online IFEA Library and Resource Center (IFEA.com) and beyond.

Moreover, without the help of some professionals and volunteers helping on this book, it would still be just a collection of notes sitting in a file drawer. I'd especially like to thank the parade chairs who reviewed the early manuscripts. Plus the IFEA in Boise, Idaho, its staff and so many IFEA members who contributed to this book; and the many individuals who sent me their suggestions and experiences with their successful parades to include in this book.

Please know that I have received no compensation from any individual, association or business mentioned throughout the book. I just believe in them and I think they have added value to you, the reader. I am very thankful for their contributions to this book.

INTRODUCTION

Is there an "expert" in this industry? Isn't every parade unique? This book, the only one of its kind to focus on improving community parades, is written for anyone responsible for or part of one of the forty to fifty thousand parade committees just in the U.S alone. It is written to share parade issues, to exchange ideas and plant a few seeds. More importantly, it is to help you take your parade beyond your current imagination or expectations.

Do you want to grow your parade, upscale it or polish it, make it more professional or tweak it? Is your goal to attract more volunteers, revenue and entries? With the number of parades shrinking due to financial considerations, having a better and more polished parade—year after year—will ensure you maintain or expand your entries, sponsors and spectators. Don't wait until those numbers start falling. *Now* is the best time to improve your parade.

In this book you'll discover the A to Z's of starting, running and polishing a community parade. Whether you are new to the endeavor or have been at it for a while, you will find tips, ideas and problem solvers here. But the world of parades is huge and no single book can incorporate every practical idea, although that is my eventual goal.

Not only will your parade's improved stature become the envy of others, you'll be a stronger political force. Especially if you deliver a parade that includes these characteristics:

- The media, community leaders, schools, clubs and businesses are involved as never before.
- The entries appreciate the improved exposure it brings in the form of more business, membership and awareness.
- The spectators love your parade because it's more innovative, exciting, fun and enjoyable.
- Spectators start bringing additional friends and family members to your parade in following years.
- Many consider your parade to be as important as their family vacation.
- It has become a tradition.
- More people from outside your community start attending.
- Your spectators start reserving more and more places to sit.
- A spectator afterward says, "That was a real parade!"

This book is not intended to be a textbook. Rather, it is designed to be an organized potpourri of useful ideas, examples, and suggestions to stimulate your creativity and encourage you to explore new ways to produce a parade.

HOW TO USE THIS BOOK

I suggest you read through the entire book and make notes to yourself. Use color to highlight those sections or ideas that have the greatest potential for your parade and may be areas to concentrate on. Be sure to make a photocopy of the table of contents to use in planning and organizing.

This book is designed to provide information on producing a parade. It is sold with the understanding that the publisher and author are not engaged in rendering legal or accounting services. If legal or other expert assistance is required, the services of a competent professional should be sought

It is not the purpose of this manual to reprint all the information that is otherwise available to parade committees, but instead to complement, amplify and supplement the few texts that already exist. You are urged to read all available material on parades you can find, learn as much as possible about running a parade and tailor the information to your individual needs.

The author is not an expert on parades and freely admits many of the suggestions are his opinions. Moreover, reasonable efforts have been made to make this guide as complete and accurate as possible, but inaccuracies have a way of slipping in. Therefore this edition of the book should be used only as a general guide and not as the ultimate source on running a parade.

Readers are asked to exchange information and their experiences and opinions with the author or on the Community Parades Facebook page, which will be incorporated into a second, more definitive edition.

The purpose of this guide is to educate. The author and Diamond Publications shall have neither the liability nor responsibility to any person or entity with respect to any loss or damage caused, or alleged to have been caused, directly or indirectly, by the information contained in this book.

TIP: Photocopy these contents pages to use in organizing your next parade.

CONTENTS

1. TAKE AN OBJECTIVE LOOK AT YOUR PARADE...... 17

2. PREPARATION FOR YOUR PARADE 46

6. PARADE STAGING 105

7. JUDGING PARADE ENTRIES 112

MISCELLANEOUS 116

APPENDICES 119

1. TAKE AN OBJECTIVE LOOK AT YOUR PARADE

Putting together a parade is like making a movie—what you have is a bunch of short clips. The goal is to take the child sitting on that curb to a different world every fifteen seconds. Once you have done this, the adults will follow simply by looking at the faces of the children.

Cody McNutt, former summer event coordinator for the
Arvada, Colorado, Harvest Festival Parade.

How about your parade? Is your parade like a movie? Does it captivate children and adults with visual scenes and drama from beginning to end? Do they leave with smiles on their faces and can't wait until next year?

If not, you have some work to do. All parades can use improvement. But where do you start?

Educate Yourself

Being the committee chair or organizer for a parade is a terrific honor and also a huge challenge and responsibility. Parades by their very nature are not static, as you are finding out. You are constantly learning. Not necessarily reinventing the wheel but improving it.

Start with yourself. Are you as knowledgeable about parades as you could be? If you haven't already done so, join your state's or a neighboring fair, festival and or event association. Contact the International Festival Event Association at IFEA.com for an up-to-date list of events in your state. (See Resources at the back of this book.) Go to their conventions, buy their books or borrow them from your local library, attend their conferences and take the web classes they offer. Make your association's parade chapter stronger by taking an active role. Ask other parade committees to join the association. Instead of trying to start your own parade organization, these associations are already built for you.

Find other parade committees in your area. Invite them to meet with you to exchange ideas. Ask to audit their meetings. Invite them to yours to show good faith and they will add all kinds of extra value. The things they take for granted might be the ones that are huge for you.

Photocopy the Table of Contents of this book as an outline you can use for discussion. Learn from searching YouTube, Facebook, Twitter and Google if you're so inclined. YouTube, for example, shows a range of parades, from Disneyland down to the Litchfield New Hampshire Truck Parade. Watch other parades for ideas.

Obtain another copy of this book for other committee members. Each reader will stimulate even more ideas for your parade. Compare notes and brainstorm together as to what enhancements you want to implement. Stretch your thinking and new opportunities will unfold.

Go to Community Parades on Facebook for more ideas, plus add your own ideas and thoughts. Email me your questions to Ed@CommunityParades.com.

Get inspired by the IFEA Pinnacle Awards. This yearly competition, called the IFEA/Haas & Wilkerson Pinnacle Awards, recognizes the outstanding accomplishments of festivals and events around the world. Why not learn from the experiences of others? Recently there were over five hundred entries from large events in 69 different categories. The classifications included four different price points. Under $250K, $250K to $750K, $750K to $1.5M over $1.5M. Reviewing several years of those awards that are of interest to your committee will offer up a gold mine of knowledge to improve your parade.

How to learn volumes from them? Ask each committee member to read several of the entries that are important to you and invite everyone to share their notes at your next meeting or special idea-sharing meeting. You are not too small a parade to learn from this feedback. Just remember, everyone has the same problems, just on a different scale.

Here's the full list of the 69 categories in the Pinnacle Awards, to show the variety and scope that is possible.

Grand Pinnacle

The Grand Pinnacle is the IFEA's highest award, reflecting the best overall festival or event in the world, within each budget category

Television & Radio

Best TV Promotion (Ad Spot or PSA)
Best Full Length TV Promotion (Local Promotion)
Best Full Length TV Program (National Promotion / Syndication)
Best Event Video (For Sale)
Best Radio Promotion

Multi Media

Best Event Website
Best Organization Website
Best Event/Organization E-Newsletter
Best Miscellaneous Multimedia (Includes, but is not limited to items such as: Screen Savers, Live Web-casts, Electronic Billboards, etc.)
Best Social Media Site
Best Festival/Event Mobile Application

Bound / Multiple Page Entries

Best Event Program (Interior 3 or less colors)
Best Event Program (Interior 4 or more colors)
Best Newspaper Insert/Supplement
Best Promotional Brochure (4 or more colors)
Best Event/Organization Newsletter
Best Miscellaneous Printed Materials (Includes but not limited to: direct mail pieces, cookbooks, annual reports, etc.)

Single Page Entries

Best Promotional Poster (Not for Sale—Used for promotional purposes to promote your event)
Best Commemorative Poster (For Sale at event)
Best Cover Design
Best Single Newspaper Display Ad
Best Single Magazine Display Ad
Best Ad Series
Best Event Photograph
Best Miscellaneous Printed Materials (Includes but not limited to fliers, maps, etc.)
Best Outdoor Billboard
Best Event Invitation (Single & multiple page invitations accepted in this category)
Best Street Banner

Sponsorship/Fund Raising

Best Sponsor Solicitation Video
Best Sponsor Solicitation Package
Best Sponsor Follow-Up Report
Best Sponsor
Best New Fundraising Program
Best Single New Sponsorship Program
Best Overall Sponsorship Program
Best Sponsorship Program for an Individual Sponsor

Community Relations

Best Environmental Program
Best Volunteer Program
Best Educational Program
Best Event/Program within an Event to Benefit a Charity
Best Community Outreach Program
Best New Promotion
Best Event (Within an Existing Festival)
Best New Event
Best Children's Programming

Best Public Safety/Security Plan for an Event

Media Relations
Best Press/Media Kit
Most Creative/Effective News Stunt
Best Media Relations Campaign

Merchandise
Best T-Shirt Design (no collared or long-sleeve shirts)
Best Pin or Button
Best Hat
Best Other Merchandise
Best Miscellaneous Clothing
Best New Merchandise
Best Overall Merchandizing Program

For Suppliers or Associations
Best Single Display Ad
Best Company Image Pieces (Includes but is not limited to: letterhead, envelopes, logo, etc.)
Best Direct Mail Piece or Brochure
Best Vendor/Supplier
Best New Product or Service

Educational Institutions Offering Event Management Programs
Best Two Year Event Management Degree
Best Four Year Event Management Degree
Best Event Management Certification Program
Best On Line Event Management Training Program
Best Festival & Event Management Master's Program
Best Festival & Event Management Program

And finally...

Just For Fun
Best Promotion Publicizing a IFEA/Hass & Wilkerson Pinnacle Award Win

Your Feedback

"California/Nevada Festivals and Events Association (CalFest) is a great resource for networking, sharing of ideas and educational opportunities for your parade planning. Many parade organizations in California are members of CalFest and are always sharing their experiences. From small town and ethnic parades and regionally and nationally televised parades, all great resources for any size parade you may have in your community."

Ray Pulver CFEE
San Jose, California
President California/Nevada Festival and Event Association.
Upbeat Parade Productions

Use an Organizational Chart

Few parade committees have one. Operating as a team is a must. If you are all going in a different direction, you are bound to falter sooner or later. Create an organizational chart, no matter how small you are. Even a one-person committee can benefit from seeing all the tasks in perspective.

Each area of focus usually calls for one person in charge. Make them a chair. Give this person the freedom to take control and full responsibility for his or her area. Be sure to delegate, not abdicate. See **Appendix A** for ideas for parade chair titles.

Once you have designated chairs, your focus will increase and the burden of trying to remember everything will lessen. Aren't you amazed how many chairs you already have?

An organizational chart is a great mechanism to take better control or improve your leadership position. Later you will discover how this also contributes to reducing your political in-house fighting, which can get out of hand without leadership.

Several areas could be chaired by the same person. Giving someone ownership and titles not only makes *you* look better, he or she will deliver more than you know. Farming out each area allows you to focus and work on any weaknesses.

Don't simply look for an assistant; find fifteen of them, each taking the most appropriate chair position. Most chair position responsibilities are small. But that is what makes it work. No one person has a lot to do. When you have each chair perfecting his or her details of the parade, you improve your parade. They feel as if they are contributing without feeling overwhelmed or insecure about continuing.

Create your own list of chairs. Add the names of the people who are currently doing it. If you don't feel you can rely on the current person doing it, show him or her your organizational chart and listen to see or ask if there is anything he or she would rather do.

Gain Respect and Credibility

If some of your sub-chairs are empty, when you distribute your organizational chart to civic groups, ask if they know of someone who would have interest in any of these areas. Let them know that you need two people per chair. Notice how they react to your organizational chart by giving you more respect.

Beyond gaining respect, the organizational chart gives your parade, its volunteers and you more credibility. This helps when you're seeking sponsors as it shows that you know what you're doing and you're not just another small-town parade, even if you are one. It simply sets you apart and allows you to focus.

Take a look at the longevity of your chairs. Are they burned out or in a rut? Has it been more than eight, twelve or twenty years? Is it time for reflection on this subject? Have they gone as far as they can go? What can you do to excite your people? One way is to provide them a copy of this book and encourage them to add their ideas.

Rotate the most experienced chair every two years. This allows for needing less control of a chair and reduces the challenges of volunteers who take too much control from you and are unwilling to change or adapt to new policies.

Remember, an organized parade makes happier participants and spectators.

Set Time Lines

Assign time lines for all tasks. List them for every component or need of the parade. The more you use time lines, the more you will feel comfortable about your current status. Get your chairs to use them routinely as well, to keep them on track.

No task is off-limits for a time line, including the all-important one of finding better entries. There's nothing that will diminish your parade quality like rushing to find entries before deadline because you didn't set an adequate time line for this project or for the entry to prepare.

Define Your Parade's Purpose

Have you given thought to your goal? Is your parade a Rodeo, Community,

Commercial, Appreciation, Boat, River, Novelty, Kids, Homecoming, Animal, Lighted, Military, Celebration, Victory, Pet, Cultural, Holiday, Political, Specialty, Religious, Ethnic, Night, Fire Brigade, Carnival, Social Statement event or another? Even the Space Shuttle Endeavor was paraded through Inglewood, California.

Every parade needs a fully defined purpose. Each one has a reason to exist. Once your improved definition is announced, the public instantly gets a better, clearer picture and you get more supportive appreciation.

Your Feedback

> "I take people out of their regular daily lives for just a moment and drop them into a world of celebration, family, friends and amazement."
>
> **R. Tony Smith**
> Marketing Director for the Cherry Creek Arts Festival, Denver, CO
> Author of numerous articles including, "Why am I in This Business? Please Remind Me!"

If the parade's purpose is to show off government entries, that is fine. If you charge local clubs, schools and charities, many entries will not come and you will be creating a Commercial Parade. If you don't charge, then you will easily attract more entries. But be careful, free entries can reduce the quality of your parade unless your parade rules maintain its integrity.

Ask Yourself...

Do you want your parade to increase its prestige by being more exciting, entertaining, interesting and to also attract more bands and musical entries? How about more scouts, community groups, houses of worship, clubs, dance and gymnastic groups, military or inflatable's? Isn't each of these usually the better community entries that entertain the spectators? Would more local, regional or national corporate entries help? Do you want your parade to be the best in its class in your region, state or beyond? All of this can be done—with forethought, planning, focus and a few more volunteers.

What experience do you want your spectators to have? Are they bored during the parade or mesmerized? Are they delighted or simply happy because they don't know how much better you *can* make it? Do the spectators look forward to it or are they there because their child is in it? Do you want the whole community to support you?

Ask What Your Elected Leaders Think

Don't take them for granted; ask them. You may learn that they didn't think much about the parade, one way or the other. Why? Because they usually ride in it and therefore never see it. Because they don't know what impact on the community it has. They don't realize its about civic pride, spirit building, community identity, image building and the new visibility it is bringing to the community and how it can bring people together. They don't see how it can lead to an improved quality of life for the spectators and the participants.

Even if you are small, you can still put together a simple, economic impact statement for them. Canvas the local restaurants on the parade route and ask what impact the parade has on them.

For a Good Perspective, Take a Look Back

Most people have no idea what it takes to make it all happen. Is yours the crown jewel or the social event of the year in your community? It can be.

For starters, is your parade well defined? Try using additional adjectives in your parade's slogan to help. The Arvada Harvest Festival Parade slogan is "Becoming the Best Community Parade between LA and Chicago." This extra wording gives it more stature. Whatever kind of parade you have, be proud of it. This pride will rub off and become even more important as you grow.

Are you losing or gaining entries? Look back and see how many you had five years ago. Is the overall quality increasing or decreasing? Is the number of spectators rising or falling? Where are you weak?

Consider the entries you get. As you grow you will need to guide or control the entries more than you did in the past. Take a good look at who your entries are now. Who are your best ones? What makes them the best?

Count and determine the number and percentage of each type of entry. You might find that it's lopsided, or it sheds light on where you need to concentrate. This information will be useful in defending your points of view if you want changes, even if your goal is simply to double the number of quality entries.

It doesn't matter if 15 percent of your entries are the same type or over 80 percent of the entries are in for free. Knowing the statistic is what defines your parade, and gives you confidence and direction that this is the type of parade you are delivering.

Are your classifications out of date? Review each parade classification and then each entry within it. Does the unit fit the classification or improve your parade? Do these entries detract? Even routine entries can be improved. Is it time to talk to them, discourage them, eliminate them or create rules to direct them?

To un-invite some entries, make sure your parade is now set up as an invitational. Or create a maximum number of entries in a particular classification or in the parade itself. Or simply change your rules to restrict entries, using some of the ones outlined later in the book. Making your parade competitive often gets you increased quality and stature.

Create Your Vision

This is different than defining your purpose. Your unique vision is what sets you apart from all other parades and attracts more funding, volunteers, spectators and better entries.

To create your vision, take a future look at the parade. Think about how you want your parade to look a few years from now. Don't worry about how to get there, or what it costs; just create the vision. If you get into a frenzy of ideas, keep going. This is called your "end result."

> "Make your parade distinctive!" says Cathy Pate, Recreation Manager for the Greenwood Village Park and Recreation District, a speaker at the Colorado Festival and Events Convention—a parade with its own personality.

Buy into whatever you decide. Believe in it. Focusing on each point will make it stronger. Prayer or quantum physics will take over.

Writing the vision down makes it clearer and will generate even more ideas. Brainstorm it with others, listing everything, big and small.

Clearly defining your vision will energize each committee member. Ask yourselves how you can make this vision happen and the ideas will come. Do this in a safe atmosphere, where everyone is encouraged to voice their opinions.

As you read further in this book, keep an open mind to all the suggestions and ideas and adjust your vision with the new thoughts you have.

Your Feedback

"To create your vision it is important to gain trust and support of people within your community. Take stock of all around you and invite key leaders (including your local police chief) in the area to join you on a parade leadership committee to build a themed parade. It is important for you to be open to suggestions and recommendations from the group.

"To accomplish these goals, you will need a plan in place to guide your committee to meet criteria for the vision of the parade you plan to develop. Know that it may be altered somewhat as members make recommendations to include show elements they would like to see involved in the developing parade. However, you are the captain of the ship and it is up to you to make the calls for the route you take to create the parade of choice. All of this has to be accomplished with political judgment by gaining support of small and large groups on your parade committee so that it works toward the vision you had early on.

"As the parade leader, you should know more than anyone else about all preparations that go into securing a parade route involving the state and federal highway requirements, local police, county sheriff, state troopers and homeland security in order to keep your parade, its participants, viewers and route safe and secure from incident(s). You should know about music license requirements from B.M.I., A.S.C.A.P., and other companies that seek out organizations that do not include music rights and set themselves up for lawsuits. When it comes to homeland security, your police chief can be extremely helpful in advising all things considered, from the staging area to the parade ending area. A city or county attorney can be your contact with the music license companies, but only if he/she has knowledge of their requirements. Otherwise include one of their representatives to join you on your committee, along with the event insurance representative.

"Make certain all parade participants are 'parade ready' in mind, body, and spirit. This includes any type of animals you or members of your committee may want to include. All of this information will need to be discussed with your insurance agent to purchase parade/event insurance, which should protect the community and your committee from lawsuits.

"Since the terrorist attacks of September 11, 2001 the parade, special event, and entertainment industry activities have also been elevated to a different paradigm, also known as a new normal. There is no room for mistakes in the parade, special event or entertainment industries anymore, or it can cost not only your career, but your life's savings."

Judy Flanagan M.S. CFEE
Savannah, Tennessee
Professional parade, event management & entertainment industry speaker

Communicate Your Vision

After implementing your new standards, go on a speaking circuit to every club, group and PTA possible. Share what the future looks like. As you are excited, so will they be. Put your vision on your website.

Most clubs are looking for speakers. Some will give you ten to twenty minutes; others longer. Some will put you on their exclusive board of director's meeting agenda. Simply contact the chair and offer your topic. Determine the amount of time you will be given and the probable number of people in attendance for handouts. Go early and organize and conceal any props you want to use during your speech.

This exercise will bring more entries, attention, volunteers and money toward your parade. Some of these groups will sprout support instantly, others in weeks or years as they see what you're doing.

Be an avid communicator everywhere you go.

Pick Your Theme

Who develops the theme? What do your city hall, borough, village, school principal or township fathers want? How does this theme fit in with your new vision?

Decide on themes several years ahead of time so entries can plan for them well in advance. Many national entries book a year or two in advance.

Improve Your Atmosphere

What is atmosphere? It's the feeling your spectators and entries have and the warmth they feel during the parade. Atmosphere also means their experiences before, during and after the parade as they are arriving and leaving.

Your spectators come with anticipation and enthusiasm. Don't disappoint them.

What atmosphere do you now have? Take another look at the purpose of your parade. Does it inspire or make people feel good? Can you enhance the atmosphere?

Here are some ideas that will enhance atmosphere and can attract more funding, entries, volunteers and spectators.

- Ask owners of businesses along the parade route to put out flags and buntings a day or two beforehand. Maybe even around your whole community.

- Ask your parks department to place some aluminum bleachers ahead of time along the parade route on public property. This creates anticipation for the upcoming parade. A 16-foot bleacher can hold thirty people and is three or four rows up. These smaller bleachers are easier to manage than larger ones. Anything over four rows will require hand rails. Ask the parks department to set them up on a weekday and take them down on a weekday so no overtime is required.

- Ask some of the businesses if they would like to rent a small bleacher for their clients' exclusive use or even for the general public. They rent for about $275. This includes delivery, leveling and pick-up.

When you think of atmosphere, think of comfort and cleanliness. Ask the city to clean the streets and sidewalk before your event.

- Check to see if the street sweepers are able to clean up confetti, glitter or streamers. If they can, then promote with your entries. If not, in your parade rules, mention that they are forbidden.

- Portable toilets? Not right on the parade route, but visible.

- Are you allowed to paint the street? If so, make sure the paint is biodegradable and easily washes off.

- Are members of Emergency Medical Services (EMS) visible? Can they also be on a bicycle, motorcycle, ATV or golf cart to be noticed by your spectators and better serve them? Let EMS know how many people will be where, especially if you have some senior grouping. More on this later.

- Nothing can destroy atmosphere as quickly as a bunch of sponsor banners. Even though they bring in additional funding, if you have enough paid entries, you can eliminate or at least minimize the use of banners. This allows the look of your parade to become more about community and less commercial. It's also less distracting. If your sponsor wants them, limit them to a fixed number.

Another way to enhance atmosphere is by asking your emcees and other officials to adhere to a dress code, such as blazer and nice pants, or even dress in your parade's theme, colors and style. The spectators will note the effect and you gain more credibility.

- A word about street sweepers that clean up after the horses or other animals in the parade: many don't clean up as well as you might expect due to the porosity of the surface. It's better to organize the parade so the animals come later if you have a large number of animals. Although residue does add atmosphere to the parade, the entries following the horses aren't going to like it.

- Consistent use of color is a major way to maintain atmosphere. If you don't have a color standard, start one. By asking for the community's endorsement of a certain color standard, you can help create bonding as each entity works toward "everything royal blue."

Enhance Your Entries

Do you give strong guidance as to what you expect from the entries or is it left up to them? Do you encourage the entries to entertain the spectators and not just ride on a float or march?

Take a look at your favorite entries from past years. What makes them special? What is the common denominator? It may be that they are "performing" in some fashion. What would happen if you doubled, tripled or quadrupled the number of entries that were performing for your spectators?

To accomplish this, encourage your entries to perform. Encourage the use of music. Make it easy for them. For example, put gas generator rental locations on your website. On parade day, watch the magic happen. And each year you will notice a significant improvement. Of course, you aren't trying to compete with Macy's or the Tournament of Roses, but you can take your spectators to a place that they never expected.

Ask for participant/unit enthusiasm at the parade to get the spectators involved and engaged. Instead of just marching, consider also cheering, clapping and chanting to promote atmosphere and enthusiasm.

The entries will respond to your requests and will get better and better each year. They, too, want to succeed by participating in an effective way and to have a lasting impact on the spectators. They want to be recognized for being creative.

- Ask the entries to go beyond status quo entertainment with real performances.

- Ask or encourage the entries to work with the theme.

- If the entries play music, encourage it with the theme in mind.

- If you have politicians in your parade, suggest they get out and walk. But they must keep up and not slow down the parade. How special is it when a U.S. president gets out of his motorcade and walks? The convertible can stay in case your politicians get tired. But be mindful that they will often slow down the parade.

- Ask the entries to engage with the spectators.

Your Feedback

> "We have a NY state association (also area associations). It has a published rule-book that can be purchased by members. It covers mostly the sport of Fire Department racing but has a large section that covers marching for firefighters, juniors, ladies auxiliaries, equipment and bands as well."
>
> **Neil Brogan**
> Port Washington, New York

Giveaways

Remember parades are a way to escape. Your spectators want to escape for a moment in time. They want you to entertain their children and themselves, and to be reminded of great times in the past. If the spectators are not entertained, they will not come next year. You need them and they expect you to deliver.

I call free things part of the entertainment. Although many parades draw the line at allowing giveaways, others add them to their parade rules. I cover this later in the book.

Your spectators love getting free things and they cherish them and appreciate them. They also expect to get them. Free things continue a long-time parade tradition and enhance the parade. If you permit giveaways, then encourage your entries to provide them.

If you are allowing free things, make an absolute rule that nothing should be tossed or thrown. Certainly nothing should be thrown within fifty feet of the horses as it can scare them.

If whatever's given out is actually made by the unit, such as free samples, it is called sampling. Handing out a coupon is called couponing. Both of these will be covered in the funding chapter.

Most entries don't know how much candy to buy. Learn by asking the entries how much they bought last year and where along the route did they run out. Suggest that 50 percent of your spectator attendance is what is needed. If you're giving coupons, goody bags, etc., then 8 percent might be about right.

Tell your entries, via your rules, that it takes three people on each side of the street to do the dispersal and up to six people if you have a larger audience of say 20,000 or so. Running out or skipping a section of parade watchers can disappoint and even alienate them. Your entries will appreciate knowing this to avoid an embarrassment.

On occasion, rather than candy, you might encourage your entries to pass out miniature flags to create an enormous effect. Have the entries pay for and order them through you and then you can place a large order for quantity discounts. Assign a block for each entry to pass them out to so everyone gets one and not five each for the initial spectators.

Reviewing Stands

For electricity, walk the parade route to see which houses or businesses have outdoor electrical outlets and ask permission to use them. While most insurance policies cover the tripping hazard, be sure to tape down the wires to avoid injury. Use rental 1,000- to 2,000-watt gas generators when no power is available and make sure you get instructions on using them. Often they quit working due to operator error.

Pick places to put the reviewing stands according to the parking that is available as that will be your largest spectator areas. Rent sound equipment from a professional rental agency or borrow the equipment from the schools. The equipment must have enough wattage to be effective. We found that the Mackie SRM 450v2 worked well.

Remember to put the speaker as high as the tripod will allow. Height improves the distance the sound can travel. Two unidirectional dynamic microphones should be considered. Borrow or rent professional-style CD or DVD players and a mixer. Our rental cost was $112 per reviewing stand.

Use the aforementioned equipment as your equivalency guide, because this is an outdoor event. This type of equipment is being stressed here because it is often overlooked and, without good sound, everyone will be disappointed.

Just One Reviewing Stand?

All spectators like to be near your reviewing stand to hear all about the entries and other commentary. Why not add more stands? We grew to fifteen, one on each block, and heard that it was one of the best new features. At least consider adding more than one. Maybe one reviewing stand per 1,250 spectators?

When you are adding reviewing stands to your parade, announce and advertise that fact beforehand. You are demonstrating "new and improved" and this will help to attract more entries and spectators. Extra reviewing stands give you more opportunity to promote the entries and your sponsors. Everybody wins. It adds value to the parade, the spectators and the entries. This means more attendance, sponsors and higher entry fees if you want this.

The Emcees Make the Parade

Invite Mr. Personality and Ms. Charming to be your volunteer emcees. Put two on each reviewing stand. That way they can work off each other and one can prep for the upcoming unit while the other is talking about the current unit going by.

Invite a police chief, city attorney, a couple of radio personalities, clergy, your school principals and superintendent, local doctors and insurance agents to be emcees. This promotes "parade envy" and other "VIPs" will want to get involved next year. Since you will lose some to attrition, keep your parade energized by inviting new business people and leaders each year to pick up the slack.

Your selection of emcees says a lot about you. Pick wisely. Reposition your best ones yearly so they don't get attached to "their spot." Don't position them in front of their own business or school; you are not supporting personal promotion. In addition, in future years always team a new emcee with one from the year before. Let everyone know that personal promotion is not acceptable beyond their occasional introductions.

Offer your emcees a brief training session a few days before the parade so they know what is expected of them.

Your Grandstand Emcees

Everybody wants someone from the local TV station to be their emcee. The spectators don't care. They simply want someone to entertain them. It can be any number of unknowns.

Be sure to communicate to each emcee that the spot is not his or hers indefinitely. It's a one year cherished position and like a U.S. presidential cabinet term, has a starting and ending point. Most are retained. This also reminds them that it's an honor to do it and an honor to be chosen once again.

To invite a television personality, check with the assignment desks at your local stations. Occasionally one of the personalities lives in your community or might just welcome having the experience to add to their resume. They are tough to get because they do so much outside work as it is. Even if you are unable to bring a personality or anchor on board, you might get some free publicity from the inquiry. Often this talent requires compensation or it's part of their contract with the station to do some free community work.

Unit Scripts

Require each unit to supply you with a typed script of forty-five words (equaling 15 seconds) for the emcee's use. It can be a description of their unit, its history, even a list of the names of people riding on the float, including band leaders. To avoid mispronunciation of names, ask them to spell difficult names as they sound. Decide if your parade's purpose allows for actual commercials. Let them know that you will edit the information for time and content, but they should strive for writing something entertaining and enticing.

Here are our two examples of scripts.

For a civic club:

> *Who likes Camping, Bows and Arrows, and Pinewood Derby Cars? Here comes the Boy Scouts! The Boy Scouts of America celebrates its 100th anniversary of providing programs that help families teach character, leadership, and citizenship. Grab a flyer and join the next century of Scouting.*

For a commercial group (the parade theme was *Music Man*):

> *Join Our Band and Make Music! Colorado Mortgage Alliance—In Tune with your Mortgage Needs—RE/MAX Alliance Arvada and Denver West Offices—Supporting Your Community!*

Be prepared to make follow-up phone calls or email the units requesting improvements to their scripts or a rewrite. Set a deadline, and if there's no response then create one for them from the entries website.

♦♦♦

Here is a sample of what some televised parades ask for, which can be useful in any parade:

TV—Master of Ceremonies Narration Information

The Anheuser-Busch Washington Birthday Parade office and parade committee is not responsible for obtaining descriptions of your unit for use by Masters of Ceremony and TV anchors. Scripts can be emailed to ______ or submitted on a labeled CD using Microsoft Word. Include all information that merits announcing (e.g., major awards, titles, drum majors, mascot, school colors and fundraisers.) Please limit your scripts to the maximum of one paragraph or one hundred twenty-five (125) words. Scripts will not be accepted after ______.

Your parade script will only be accepted on disk or via email. The parade is limited to a ninety-minute broadcast so every entry selection can be competitive. Entries will be selected based on entertainment value, originality, design concept, adherence to the theme...

♦♦♦

Pre-Parade Entertainment

Once the street is closed you have hundreds or thousands of people sitting on the curb waiting. Some will be waiting for a few minutes and others for an hour or more depending on where they sit and the length of your parade route.

Your goal is to make the pre-parade entertainment so good that they come for that and the parade is a bonus.

With reviewing stands you can offer music. Find top dance songs and watch your spectators react and get off the curb. Don't be afraid of some of the old but fondly remembered classics, like conga lines, the bunny hop, the electric slide or the Macarena. Invite local square dance clubs or ballroom dance studios to perform and to encourage more participation. Also ask cheerleader groups, singers, musicians and choirs to perform. Or simply use classic marching band and patriotic music.

Your emcees can provide background on your event. Suggest simple contests or use trivia and jokes to entertain the spectators. Make available to them gifts, like a lottery ticket, for the spectators to win for best dancing. Provide them a handout on the history of your parade and the community. Include interesting details and a list of the entries and their commentary. Here is a good example of parade history.

Your Feedback

"Carnival in Nice, France is probably the oldest continuing event in the world, dating back at least 1,000 years. It was also the original pre-Lenten carnival, of which there are now hundreds in the world.

"Therefore, all carnival/Mardi Gras events, including Mardi Gras in New Orleans, have their origins in the Carnival in Nice. For years, event managers borrowed ideas to begin their new events through a process known as 'networking.'

"One of the featured events in Nice during this time was the Battle of Flowers Parade, which featured floral floats that went up one side of the Promenade d'Anglais, and then turned around and went down to the other side, twice. On the second time around, float riders threw the flowers that adorned the float into the crowd.

"In 1889, when it was a just a shade under 900 years old, a man from Pasadena, California was at Carnival in Nice. He returned home and told friends, 'Pasadena should have an all-floral parade like that one.' That was, arguably, how the best parade in the world, the Pasadena Tournament of Roses Parade, was born.

"Those who have been to Mardi Gras parade in New Orleans know that float riders throw plastic beads into the crowd of people, many of whom fight with frenzy for the 'throw.' It is thought that the idea of throwing flowers, as was done at the Battle of Flowers Parade, was transformed into the throwing of beads in New Orleans.

"In addition to those mentioned here, hundreds of pre-Lenten Carnivals, including Carnival in Rio de Janeiro, Brazil and the Battle of Flowers Parade, which is part of Fiesta San Antonio each April, came out of Carnival in Nice."

Bruce Skinner CFEE
Portland Washington
Author with Rukavina and Goldblatt of the book,
The Complete Guide to Event Sponsorship

Ask a state officer in the local Toastmasters chapter to chair this meeting if you need to.

Ask the emcees to bring their own card table and chairs. Suggest also bringing a 10 foot X 10 foot canopy. The canopy can be very helpful to identify their location for the parade entries and the spectators, and also to keep everything dry. To obtain some for your emcees, you might contact a store like Checker Auto Parts, which offers a basic one for about $50. Civic clubs and houses of worship might have them available for your use as well. Your emcees will be well served if there is a way to elevate them a foot or more above the sidewalk by obtaining two-foot rentable stages. The audience and the units passing by will appreciate being able to identify where the emcees are located. We are experimenting with 4 foot x 6 foot flags used as banners.

Don't leave the choice of attire up to the emcees, or you will be disappointed. This apparel is to distinguish not only themselves to the crowd but for the police to be able to identify who is who if needed if a problem arises.

Beforehand, contact the school principals for help in asking the children to write thank-you notes and hand them out to the inactive/retired/active military, fire, police, and ambulance "spectators" during the pre-parade entertainment. Ask local Cub Scout troops to hand them out. A scout leader with a bull horn or the emcees can ask the members of the audience to raise their hand if they have been members of the military, etc.

Pass Out the Chalk

It's cheap and will be an instant hit. Don't think that the children will only use the chalk to draw around their curb area. They and even their parents will go into the street and draw all kinds of things. You may even be creating a family bonding moment that is priceless.

Use white chalk if you have black top, asphalt or macadam; a bright colored chalk (not pastel) if you have concrete streets. Break the chalk in half to go further if you are coming up short. It's cheaper to order one color in large quantities as compared to smaller quantities with lots of colors. Do not offer multi-colored chalk as children can't make up their mind or will want one of each.

You might consider using dustless chalk. An acquaintance of mine, Marcia Reece, told me about it. She and her children created it decades ago and sold it to a major toy manufacturer. Using dustless chalk might reduce a post-parade dry cleaning bill.

Balloons

Put helium tanks at each reviewing stand and offer free or free sponsored balloons. Imagine your parade route lined with balloons. Be sure to order balloons that accept helium and are eco-friendly. Order early; as of this writing, helium is being rationed. See the chapter on sponsors for more ideas.

Military

I asked our Mayor to write a letter to the Governor to invite two generals in the Colorado Air National Guard and a BlackHawk to come to the event.

They were going to land in Olde Town Arvada, pick up the two generals and drop each one off on fields across from two of the reviewing stands, take off, land in Olde Town and set up a static display at the festival. The generals' cars were close to Olde Town.

It's a lot of work and sometimes the pilots are in training during your event, making it even tougher. The pilots will come by the day before to inspect the landing sites. We showed them where the bands were staging at a local theater parking lot and where the rest were staging along a mile-long street. We also let them know where the horses were.

Everything was dramatic and memorable. You will be in constant contact and told when they take off from their field, when they will arrive, and not only when the Generals are ready to leave, but which way they are going to take off and circle one time for pictures, On takeoff, the copilot stood outside the air craft and gave the crowd huge waves.

You will need the fire department to stage at the sites just like they do at Flight for Life landings. We also asked some of the spectators to help, just to add to their adrenaline.

To accomplish something like this, contact and meet your State Deputy Public Affairs Officer and your state National Guard. This also applies to flyovers, etc.

Support Your Spectators

As mentioned, ask all of your entries to perform for the spectators in some way. The entries will be appreciative because they want to be seen as community supporters and they need your guidance. You can reinforce getting more performance from your entries by emphasizing it in your judging qualifications.

Your Feedback

"With regards to creativity/innovation:
The experience of your stakeholders (audience, sponsors, participants, etc.) is only going to be **memorable** if your next parade stands out from previous parade experiences. To do so, you should consider changing or improving any of the building blocks that make your parade. In other words, rethink how you do things, what can be replaced, added or left-out.

Example:
A meta building block is that the audience is standing along the route watching parade entries pass by. Now let's rethink...One line of thought is to have the audience pass by parade entries where the floats are stationary. This could translate into ending the parade in a stadium or field so the audience could walk around the floats and look at them in detail.

Another line of thought would be: Could the floats be facing the people standing along the route? This could translate into the idea to motivate your audience and businesses along the route to decorate.

Cameras on one of your floats could record the whole route on both sides. The video streams could be available online (creating traffic to your website after the parade, when the audience is viewing the other side of the parade and looking for their moment of fame...) and could be projected on video screens by your grandstand. You could ask all your parade float participants to judge sections of the route and you have a whole new awards category."

Jeroen Mourik
Icod de los Vinos, Spain
Author of "RSS Feeds for Festivals," "Events in Germany United the World, ""New Festival City Program" and "Becoming Effective in Creating Innovative Ideas"

How Many Days?

Many parades with a festival run daily over a period of a week or so. Is this something you should be doing or, alternatively, should you be cutting down on the number of days?

Applaud Your Retirees

Contact the activity directors at senior recreation centers and independent living complexes. Let them know that you will create special reserved seating for their residents and patrons and special access for their buses. Get permission for their vans to go through a school field or locked commercial site along the parade route and deliver them right to the curb through an unlocked gate. If the field ground is wet, put down sheets of plywood for the wheel chairs up to the sidewalk. Our city, for instance, provided three bleachers holding thirty people each. The parks department provided the chairs.

If you have to pay for bleachers and have no sponsor, the seniors can be asked to pay a $10 fee to cover its cost.

There may be a senior resource police officer within your jurisdiction who has contact with these groups. Ask if he or she would serve as your senior chair-person.

Many activity drivers don't work on Saturdays. But once the word gets out, seniors will urge their activity directors to participate. The residents will talk about this for weeks before and after and, since you promoted this effort, you will become a hero. The community center or senior living complex will get high marks for including your parade in its activities, and will be able to promote the activity to potential residents.

If the weather is hot, the seniors in particular may require shade. Unless you can provide shade with an awning or tent, or a sponsor can, let them know they will need to dress accordingly.

Get a Banner

Measure the width of your street. It's typically ten feet per lane. Shorten the banner to allow at least five feet of clearance on both sides of the street so as not to interfere with the spectators on the sidelines. A shorter banner or less expensive one is better than no banner.

This alone will win the hearts of your spectators. It adds excitement, is a unique feature and sets you apart from the rest.

How We Did It...

For our parade, we ordered a 30 foot x 3 foot vinyl banner as we have a quarter mile parade street with a width of 21.5 feet and then a mile of the parade route width of 50 feet. The banner was a huge hit. We folded back some of the banner, allowing only the name of the community to show in the narrow quarter mile stretch, until they rounded the corner showing the full width of the banner. The price was $1,100. This included hardware, such as removable rods and twenty pole-pocket hand holds along the top for ten people and a smaller rod along the bottom to maintain the banner's integrity, shape and rigidity. You could also mount this elsewhere for display for your other events or use it for advertising before or after your event by adding grommets.

We decided on a colorful background. Most banners simply have a one-color background and the title. Not sure why, other than simplicity and contrast to make the title stand out. I think the price might be about the same if you are using four (full) colors.

To keep the sun from shining through during the parade, a vinyl banner with a thick backing can be used. It should have a long shelf life assuming you store it and roll it up properly over a tube with the banner facing out.

You can see it at the CommunityParades.com website.

Entertain and Thank Your Entries

Even though the entries enjoy being in a parade, it is a lot of work. To make sure they want to come back next year, why not post a sign, a clown or even yourself at a position just before the parade route and thank each group for coming? We do it personally and we have also hired an eighteen-foot-tall human puppet to wave, bow and applaud each unit (costume from Stretch's Lair, GiantPuppet.com) who goes to many parades in our sixteen-state region. We tell each unit thanks for coming, that the puppet is there to entertain you because you are about to entertain the spectators. The puppet then joins the parade at the end. Participants get a lot out of being in the parade, but being thanked in this manner is special and memorable.

We also tell the entries that twenty thousand people are waiting to see you around the corner. That message is usually inspirational but occasionally negative as one entry suggested that it would make the stress worse for the kids.

Have someone board each school band bus before it leaves to thank them for coming. Let the students know that it was their director and others who made the event possible to attend.

Support Your Entries

Your goal is to get "buy in" from the entries and to reduce any parade, line-up and staging irritations. In addition, you will need to provide encouragement, instill a sense of belonging and show how their involvement fosters community camaraderie.

Your acceptance notifications need to be sent out as quickly as possible to facilitate the entries getting the budget through, finding the volunteers or staff and building their floats to keep their momentum going, and to not lose interest.

Furthermore, telling the entries their staging number and time two weeks before parade day helps them to inform and contact those within their groups, eventually letting the student participants know and also the parents.

There is often a larger chain of communication that needs to take place in a timely manner than most parade committees realize. If you're getting calls inquiring about where to line up, then you may need to distribute the information at an earlier date.

Your Feedback

> "Consider setting up an RSS Feed with your up-to-date line-up (take out the cancelled and *no-show* entries before the start of the parade) and another RSS Feed in relation to the winners in the various judging categories. Everyone who subscribes to these feeds has direct access to the latest info. A mobile phone app could be created to publish the info of the two feeds to members of the public with smart phones. Your web designer can use the same feeds to automatically publish the latest info directly on your website. An Internet savvy person should be able to do this on a shoe-string budget if needed."
>
> --Also from Jeroen Mourik

Other ways to support your entries...

Is your judging on a flat street? Many bands and other entries will struggle trying to stay in step after going up or down a small hill or incline.

Politicians

If politicians are paying a large premium for their entry, have your emcees, during the pre-parade entertainment, tell the audience that these political entries are helping to pay for the parade. Ask the spectators beforehand to stand up for them and applaud. The politicians will be surprised and might say that they have never been treated better. We had one senator fly in for the weekend from Washington while Congress was in session, just for the parade. It was his third continuous attendance. You can also use this same approach on sponsors or other paid entries you want to give special recognition to.

Websites that Shine

For example, here is a sampling of what the San Diego Pride Parade website includes. Their parade kit is twenty pages and is a good resource for you or your committee to review.

How Do You Become a Real Show Stopper?

- A routine of choreographed movement
- 1-2 minute looped music track
- Fabulous costumes
- Coordinated story or message

Floats

Floats are excellent entertainment and a fun way to show off your organization. Floats can easily express your enthusiasm and can be an effective way to promote your message, leaving a lasting impression. Floats can be built on trailers, trucks, cars, hay wagons, and flatbeds. You need a flat, secure surface attached to four wheels and an axle with framework. It needs to be safe for riders, meaning you must have secure poles or equivalents that the rider can hang on to, if the need should arise.

Many groups start fundraising for their spectacular floats in January. Budget properly and keep in mind, that all floats are crowd pleasers. A creative, well thought out, colorful and safe float can be effective.

Here are two online manuals on how to build a float at www.victorycorps.com:
The How-To-Do-It for the Amateur Float Builder, 16 pages
Everyone Loves A Parade! The Authoritative Guide on How to Plan, Start & Improve Your Local Parade, 136 pages

Your Feedback

"We recommend to our customers that they measure accurately all products before they order float materials. Many times we see customers ordering additional supplies at the last minute in a rush."

Ellen
Shindigz.com South Whitley Indiana

Tricks of the Trade

Enlarge the effective size of your unit through movable extensions such as people, flags, fabric, streamers, fans, bubbles or balloons. Remember to keep extensions retractable so you can safely negotiate the route.

Don't have the time? Don't have any float ideas…but have a budget? Contact me and let's discuss other options.

Homecoming Parades

Your Feedback

"Little parades, mid-size parades and large ones. In many ways they are the same.

- Seek out sponsors, especially local food vendors, who can help offset food and beverage expenses with in-kind donations or new revenue.
- Think of ways to involve as many community members as possible in the parade to increase attendance (e.g., is there a school marching band that can march in the parade or a sports team with their mascot?).
- What is the WOW factor? Fireworks? A really big or animated float? A celebrity appearance? What is the one thing that people won't want to miss and will be the deciding factor for them to come?
- Come up with your inclement weather cancellation criteria well ahead of time and how you will communicate that message if you need to at the last minute.
- Make sure all of your volunteers have clear expectations and responsibilities, and have all of the contact information (cell phone lists, radios) they need.
- If your parade runs into the evening, light the route with portable

rental lights to ensure everyone can see the parade and make a safer environment as people are heading home."

Adam Burden
Ohio State University
Coordinator of Student Involvement

Your Feedback

"Hello, my name is Carol Perea and I am the 'parade person'...for our Homecoming at Anderson High School. We are a relatively small school, thus we do not have a committee...just myself and student helpers.

1. The value in a Homecoming Parade is what absolutely carries the event. This is a 'tradition,' one that has not been lost and means as much to our community, business and families as it does to the high school. In our last parade, we had representation from three generations of Anderson High School involved. The Grand Marshal was an alum, his daughter was a homecoming queen candidate (who later won the title), and the car in which she rode in the parade was driven by her grandfather, who was an Anderson High Alum and former teacher.

2. The students enjoy the creative spirit and create wonderful floats that represent our current theme for Homecoming and their classes or club. The class advisors assist the students in finding drivers, and trailers for the event. This brings about collaboration and conversation with the community members, parents, grandparents, students and staff. Students work with their advisor to create the floats, supplying those special things that make them unique. It is crazy hectic...but so worth the effort as everyone comes away smiling after the parade. We get a parade Permit from our local police dept., so they are aware of the time, date and number of entrants. The local fire department opens the parade with the Antique Anderson Fire Truck, and closes the parade with their current fire truck. Local community members are requested along with our Superintendent to judge the floats. It reminds us of times past and connects us to our roots. Every person who is asked to help does...because they love to see this event happen. It shares our school and our students' energy with the community. The local paper covers the event.

3. We will continue to have our Homecoming Parade...BECAUSE WE CAN! There are so many communities who are not able to have an event like this so we will keep doing it until we drop. We have had to modify some things due to new regulations (purchase fire retardant spray and

coat all paper products), meet with the fire department so they can inspect the floats prior to the parade, limit number of students who can ride on a float or in a vehicle, ensure each vehicle has a fire extinguisher.

4. Mistakes...not too many, but more planning time to allow more people to be in the event, and generate more publicity.....like create a 'committee' so we can get info out to the community at large and have more participants. A concern is to not have it get too big, so as to take too much more time. We have students who need to ride a bus home and have to have our parade finish at a specific time so they can catch the bus home. The school buses pick students up downtown as opposed to the high school, so all students have the ability to watch the parade."

Carol Perea
Anderson Union High School, Anderson, California

Your Feedback

"Keep it simple. Have a small committee of like-minded people who share your passion. While everyone has a specific job/duty, all members share in the workload together to achieve a successful outcome."

Gunther Kaschuba
Burlington Christmas Parade, Burlington, Canada

Have some ideas to share? Go to the Community Parades Facebook page and post them there.

2. PREPARATION

As you go through this book, it's easy to get caught up in the details. Here's a parade definition to help you keep the big picture in mind:

What is a parade?

> *A procession of pedestrians, vehicles or animals, or any combination thereof, traveling in unison along or upon a street, road, highway or sidewalk, organized and conducted for the purposes of attracting the attention of the general public and/or expressing or celebrating views or ideas by the use of verbal, visual, literary, or auditory means of communication.*

Getting a Permit

It's now pretty tough for a municipality or police chief to turn down a parade permit. At least that is what three recent court rulings have found in New York City, Seattle and Cincinnati. Seems like your permit will be issued if reasonable safety guidelines are met.

If you want to replace a current ongoing parade, apply for a parade permit before someone else does. However, be aware that this can bring about a host of political issues and bad feelings.

A survey of some of the uncommon parade permit language and some of my observations on applications is available in **Appendix B**.

Your Operations Manual

Yes, you must have one. Someone needs to be able to easily take over in your absence. Use the Table of Contents of this book to start your manual's outline and create it from there.

You don't need to finish it the first year. Start it before the event and then update it shortly afterward. It won't be perfect the first year, but during the second year you can perfect it. An important legacy for other parade organizers who take over is to have your reasoning and thoughts on key components.

Have each of your chairs write their job descriptions and how their side of the committee works. You don't have to do it all; just be the editor.

Your Website

Often overlooked, your website makes you more credible to the spectators, your entries and your sponsors. Add music, a weather forecast, a countdown clock, and post pictures and videos. We put a new-users counter on it. The website hits were slow in the beginning and started to rise quickly a month or so beforehand. During the last week before our parade it grew to ten thousand.

Websites are great communications tools and should contain much of your operations manual. There are many off-the-shelf websites you can use with little or no expense and a smaller learning curve as well. Paying someone thousands to create it doesn't make sense for this endeavor.

To be more polished, timely and cost-effective, work toward putting *everything* on the website. That includes applications, acceptance, rejections, parade rules and staging information. Many private matters also can be included on the website in an area that only you and who you choose can enter.

Your Feedback

"Today, the most important aspects for your website are visitor perspective and device accessibility. What information should you provide and how can it be easily viewed.

"When planning the content for your website, consider the perspective of the various audiences who will visit your website. What information are they seeking? What questions do people typically ask when they call?

"Start with the basics and put them in a prominent location:
- When is the event? The date AND the time
- Where is the event? Be sure to include all notable locations like parking, starting place, stopping place and good spots for observation, etc.
- What will be available? Are there bathroom facilities or concessions?
- Are there any rules or guidelines attendees should follow?

"After you have all of the basics covered, answer secondary questions like:
- Who is involved? Who are the event sponsors and coordinators? Is there a beneficiary?
- Are there any costs or other special considerations?
- Is there an inclement weather policy?
- Are there volunteer opportunities?

"Be sure to give visitors a way to connect with your organization. If you don't want to answer phone calls, provide an email address. Update your website with answers to questions that are frequently asked. Connection through Twitter and Facebook are great, just be sure you monitor your accounts so you can respond when people post questions or comments.

"While most visitors to your website will use a desktop or laptop computer about a third of them will use a hand-held device. Research shows that this trend will continue to grow. Be sure that your website works very well on mobile devices. If your website management system offers a mobile version be sure to use it and be sure to test it. Consider what a mobile website visitor would want to know and how this may be different than what a desktop visitor would want to know. Also be sure to take advantage of the phone's special capabilities like maps and single taps to Tweet, call or email.

"Finally, consider what a mobile user would want to know on the day of your event. Things like maps, parking information and inclement weather announcements are more important.

"By considering what your website visitors want to know and how they will try to find answers will make your website much more useful."

Jacob Savage
Memphis, Tennessee, SpeakCreative.com

Your Grandstand Location

Look for additional places, like a roof top or a balcony. Try to place the grandstand early along the parade route as the entries will become tired further down the line.

Reviewing Your Route

There may be a logical place to start and finish the parade depending on the size of your main street and other characteristics. Giving this issue extra consideration might provide some additional ideas. Because it's a tradition doesn't mean you shouldn't ponder the question of moving it. After all, Macy's changed theirs in 2009 after eighty-four years.

- Has some physical street, building, shopping center or parking lot been torn down?
- What is going to affect your future parades in the long term?
- Will streets be resurfaced or closed during your parade?

- How many blocks is it?
- How long does it take the first unit to reach the end?
- How long does it take the last unit to reach the beginning?
- Does the parade route meet your future vision goals?
- Should you increase the length to accommodate more spectators?
- Do you want the parade route shorter for better effect?

Changing the route may take some preparation and you should probably work towards doing this on the second year, planting the seed in the first year. When you do change the route, you will need to let the media, the entries and the spectators know well in advance, even the year before. Some still will not get the word and end up going to the same place. You will need signage at the old location and a volunteer there to redirect them on parade day.

Try these:
A rule of thumb might be the length of the parade route equals the length of the entries. If you have one-half mile of entries in staging, you might need one-half mile of parade route.

Another rule might be the number of spectators. If it's weak, then shorten your route to increase the effect.

Look for tree branches and overhead wires along the parade route. Certainly there is an immediate discussion with your streets department if tree limbs hit semis. Some of these problems can be handled over time simply by asking.

Power Lines

For example, our community has twelve power lines over the 1.25-mile parade route. We asked the city to bury them. Our metro area electrical company puts a percentage of its budget into a fund to pay for this. Check with your electrical provider and see what options you have. Make sure the telephone and cable lines will be rerouted if the electrical line is buried. You don't want the pole to remain standing. Removing them also reduces traffic hazards, down power lines from a storm and creates a visually appealing street.

Often, there are additional telephone and cable wires on the power poles. If you want to raise them, the rule is that nothing can be near the electrical within 42 inches. However you can ask for a taller pole to be installed.

Typical poles are 35 feet but there are many sizes going up to 70 feet. Many of the power lines are probably a single line to the street light. Check to see if you can get it reconnected to a pole on the same side of the street.
The bottom line is you have options once you start to look into it.

Should You Go the Opposite Direction?

Wherever the entries disband has value. Do they end up at your festival or at a shopping center that will benefit? Can you circle the parade route so that the entries start and stop at the same location? Or how about going both ways? Once you arrive at the end of the street, turn around and go back down the parade route.

Faster or Slower?

Speed is important as it will define your parade. If you have gaps or the parade is too slow, that will get talked about instead of the good things.

Decisions about the speed and flow of your parade can be stated in your staging letter (see Chapter 6). Marching bands don't perform, start and stop; they march. Maintaining the same speed is critical for the bands. If you want the parade to move more quickly, your parade rules need to spell out exactly what is expected about stopping or performing. Your parade marshals can enforce them.

Caution. You can be so successful at this that it goes too fast! The spectators barely absorb one unit when another is in front of them. That's not fair to the unit or the spectators.

Speed can be determined by overall time allotted for the parade. To have a longer parade time, encourage thirty-second performance(s) from some of the best entries. To really stretch out the parade, also offer some of the remaining entries the opportunity to perform.

For performing entries that stop, determine how many seconds and where. If you don't control this facet of the parade, you will end up being surprised. Often the performances are in front of the reviewing stand and at your largest spectator locations. You may want to control this privately by reviewing your plans with the entries you have asked to perform, either in their staging letters or personally.

To help eliminate or shorten gaps, put near the top of your rules that if the entry is more then X feet away from the unit in front of them, *anywhere* along the parade route, they will be disqualified from the judging and may not be asked to return next year or put on probation. We have found that some entries do it on purpose because they believe it gains them more attention. But in reality their entry is blamed by the audience for being so slow.

What's the Best Time to Start and End?

Picking the right starting and ending times can allow the weather to work in your favor rather than against you.

What kind of weather might you expect in your region? Does the dew or fog disappear by 9 a.m.? Is the morning more likely to be drier than the afternoon? If you're an evening parade, what time does it actually get dark? When does the temperature start to really drop? Email your local weatherman to help you with these technical stats and you might even get a free plug.

Take into consideration the needs of the community. When do the children need to be finished? If they can't get to a practice or a game on time, they might not attend at all. This applies not just to elementary school age groups; bands and sports teams often have a full schedule on Saturday afternoons.

We changed our parade to start at 9 a.m. to allow for a future of longer parades and students' needs. They are done by 12:30 p.m. and then can head to the festival for lunch.

Be mindful of mealtimes. If your parade lasts beyond the noon or dinner hour you might lose attendance when the spectators get hungry.

As mentioned earlier, making changes to your parade needs careful consideration. If you are going to change your starting time, try to do it soon. Each year your parade will be growing and it's difficult to get the message out when new entries and spectators become familiar with tradition. Moving it now is easier than when you have doubled the spectator attendance.

Don't forget to make sure you are not competing with other major events that day, either in the area or on TV.

Can You Spot a Human Predator?

Uninvited vendors are those who break into your parade without your permission. Some call it gorilla marketing. These vendors are using *your* parade to sell things. What happens if a purchase turns out bad for one of your spectators? Can you see the headline? "Spectator sickened by tainted food at local parade. Parade officials blamed for careless overview of vendors." A good point.

Keep in mind, you "own" the streets during the parade. However, your parade permit by law usually may not control the sidewalks.

How about an uninvited or non-paying group showing up and handing out their coupons at your event? These predators are using your captive audience to their advantage. This type of couponing should not be allowed a free ride. Please review Chapter 3 Funding on charging them appropriate fees.

Watch for predators showing up with petitions, asking spectators to sign. This interferes with the spectators' enjoyment of your parade. It's like going to a movie and having someone interrupt you during the show.

What about those entries, paid or not, who pass out free samples? The spectators aren't getting coupons, they are getting the product. That business is reaping a huge benefit. Check the Funding section for pricing.

You're bringing the spectators, collecting income from sponsors and entries. You have built not only the attendance but a captive one at that. Your audience is very appealing to predators and it isn't fair to your paying entries and sponsors.

One way to minimize these instances is to have your approved vendors wear a special vest, hat or sticker that changes each year.

Combating Couponers, Samplers and the Uninvited

Ask them to leave.

Ask to see their special event sales tax application required for vendors from your sales tax division.

Ask to see a copy of their driver's license.

Take a picture of them with your cell phone.

Ask the police beforehand if they will throw them out.

Ask the police to run a warrant check on them.

Station a person around them to use negative body language, such as shaking their head "no" to the audience.

Let your adult parade marshals challenge them.

Use your emcees to ask the spectators to show their disinterest in such conduct. You own the microphones; use them to educate.

Request an entry fee.

Tell them they must stay on the sidewalk.

Beforehand, go to other parades and ask them what the most popular items are that they sell. (So far the number-one seller in our area is sunglasses.) Then ask your local scout troop to sell those items and wear their uniforms. The spectators will respond better to the scouts, especially if items are offered at a lower price.

Limit them to non-consumable items.

Parking

Parking can be troublesome. Put a city or Google map on your website showing where people can park. Your spectators are eager to find spots. Often there are spots you didn't think of until you spot them on an aerial map. This offers the opportunity for not only less congestion but larger attendance numbers.

Can you offer VIP or gratis parking? They will appreciate you if you put it on your website or Facebook page.

Review the video from your last parade. Note where the most and fewest people gather to watch. A large gathering often means there is parking nearby; alternatively, a sparse spectator area means a lack of close-in parking. If there is a school football field or long stretch without side streets, parking will be limited so the spectators are fewer at this location.

If parking is very limited, mention in all your announcements that you are sorry, but there is no close-in parking. This will allow spectators advance planning, time to walk and not complain about parking.

Shuttles, an Alternative to Close-In Parking

Take this option only if you can afford to. For some parades, the cost can be $10,000 to $20,000 to rent buses or vans.

First see which parking lots might accommodate a shuttle. This would include municipal buildings, houses of worship, sports fields, theaters and shopping centers.

The farther away the parking lot is the more buses you need. The spectators will want no more than a ten-minute wait.

Keep in mind that buses might need to run for several hours before and after your parade. Busing would support spectators and some parade entries as well.

To find alternative transportation, enlist the help of houses of worship, preschools and your local school district. They usually have small buses. Check to see if your parade insurance or theirs can cover it. You may be able to add a rider to your insurance to cover this type of transportation. This will be cheaper than your local bus service. Your insurance company may require a special driver's license and a State Bureau of Investigation check on each driver. You may not be able to charge a fare if this conflicts with taxi cab licensing laws.

In return for the use of the buses:

- Offer a free entry into the parade.
- Pay for the drivers.
- Pay for their fuel.
- They can be treated as an in-kind sponsor with recognition.
- Have your emcee mention how much help they are.
- Add a banner on their buses thanking them.

American Disabilities Act

Be sure you know what is needed and where. Will there be restrooms that accommodate people with disabilities? Volunteer interpreters, signers, special seating? Letting everyone know you have addressed these issues adds polish and credibility to your parade. Add a section on your website or Facebook. Offer a handout for information at your reviewing stands and note it in your publicity releases and programs.

Are You Properly Insured?

Most parade permits require a copy of your insurance policy. If you don't have insurance, it's time. Your biggest risk is horses. They hurt or kill more people in parades than any other unit. The second biggest risks are a vehicle running into another vehicle along the parade route and spectator's retrieving thrown candy from a moving vehicle.

Most policies cover you but don't cover the unit that injures someone. It's their problem. Post that fact in your application and/or parade rules.

Put out a Request for Proposal (RFP) with a couple of insurance agents for more information. Your parade permit will let you know how much insurance is appropriate, usually $1 million. For medium or more elaborate parades, you may want up $3 to $5 million.

Check with your insurance company for what rules they want instituted. Often it's a couple of breeds of dogs that are not covered. Your community may not allow certain types of dogs or other animals into the community. Add these to your parade rules. If it's an animal parade, do your homework and find out if the animal control people will be looking the other way on licensing, shots or legality. Maybe they will just give a note to a handler that their dog should see a veterinarian, if they spot something wrong.

Finding More Volunteers

As a parade chair you shouldn't and can't do it all, and if you try to, it won't get done as well as it could. Committee chairs should find and work with your assistants. You work toward improving your parade. That is your goal.

This book can't cover it all. Check out the 28 books and webinars listed on the IFEA's website. And on Amazon and elsewhere, I liked *Recruiting & Managing Volunteers* by John L. Lipp, San Francisco Bay area, California. I highly recommend reading one or more of these books on volunteering. Reading them improved my life and will yours. Did you know that more than one out of four adults volunteered their time recently? Getting volunteers is now easier. The goal of this book is to be the nation's best resource on running a parade and this is one of the areas parade committees are challenged by.

Again, don't be a control freak. Delegate, don't abdicate.

Another source for volunteers is the increasing senior population.

Often there is one civic club that is growing. They are a great resource.

Look at your organizational chart showing the individuals in charge of what and where you have openings. Contact those you know or learn about the ones who will be perfect for the position.

Many organizations ask volunteers for only two hours of their time to maximize the number of volunteers. Make each job simple.

Create a page on your website explaining your job descriptions and what volunteers get in return. You can pick up some dependable people this way. One year, we had a retired FBI agent ask if we needed help with security, with our parade marshals and our "predators."

Go to your local online Craig's List. It has a volunteers' section.

Another idea is to go online and search for volunteer organizations and see what is available locally.

And another: There are those who are forced into community service as part of a petty crime. If you're comfortable with the concept, let your local attorneys know of your needs.

Identify every organization in your community. There are more than you can imagine. Not only civic clubs, but scout groups, business groups, PTA's, bridge clubs, hospital volunteer groups, home owner associations and even book clubs. Send them a brochure seeking volunteers.

Not all volunteers will be assigned to work the actual parade. After a local garden club presentation I gave, with an attendance of forty-five, two ladies eagerly suggested that their husbands might like to help with improving the website. One of the ladies texted her husband during the event and came back right then with a yes.

When planning how you will use the volunteers, don't overwhelm them with work or their fear of failure will take over. On the other hand, don't give them so little to do that they lose interest. Be sure to give them credit for what they do and praise them.

Group Volunteers

Scout groups, volunteer fire fighters, civil air patrol and police cadets are great as parade stagers and marshals. They need community activities to support and they work in groups with their own adult supervision.

Check out high school honor societies. Often these students are particularly motivated and can be trusted to handle any number of things. Also, consider ROTC (Reserve Officer Training Corps) but they may need a small donation of financial support. Like the scouts, they create a commanding image and know how to get the job done.

Look at these organizations and see or ask who is appropriate for the single chair job you need done. It may well be a past president.

Volunteers come in all shapes and sizes. The ones who contact *you* are often the best because they are motivated and they have the expertise you need. They want to be part of a project that is fulfilling and wonderful. The more details you share with them, the more they will want to participate.

Ask for volunteers whenever you're talking to someone. Being specific about your needs helps them to understand and explain to others. Carry a list of tasks.

Don't forget looking for volunteers at the parade itself. During each parade, be sure to announce at your grandstand microphone several times that you are always looking for volunteers for next year. Tell them to come up and give their name and address or go to your announced website.

Those who are passionate for the position often prove to be a great choice. Sometimes they come at a personality price, but it's often worth it. Some of the profiles of great volunteers might be Mr. Likable, Mrs. Doer, Mr. and Mrs. Retired & Active, Mr. Chair of other things, Mrs. Person of the Year.

- The more excited you are about the parades and the openings, the more volunteers you will find.
- The better your parade is, the easier it will be to find volunteers. People want to be a part of it.
- Submit an article in the local newspapers or a letter to the editor seeking volunteers.
- Post a note on bulletin boards at recreation centers, grocery stores, online blogs, and Twitter if you're so inclined.
- As you grow, and the number of volunteers grows, schedule a volunteer meeting to inform them of their duties and give them a better understanding of the undertaking.

Your Volunteers' Compensation Package

Some volunteers don't get anything other than a thank-you or a note of thanks.

The younger they are the more appropriate it might be to give a lunch coupon, movie theater tickets, a themed T-shirt or baseball cap. Teenage volunteers love caps that have an official looking star or celebrity image on them. Or offer a luncheon, dinner or a party at a later date. Always keep in mind that the compensation to the volunteer should match the work done, but still be minimal.

Improve Your PR

Unless you are in the PR business, publicity and public relations will be one of your challenges. It also can be exciting and rewarding work.

To get the most attention, be unique...or even controversial. There are many books on how to get publicity and *Community Parades* doesn't try to compete with them. Here are just a few ideas:

- Meet with your sponsor's advertising agencies. On their radio spots, they might mention what your sponsor is doing for the community by supporting your parade.

- Ask your city or businesses to put a promotion for your parade in their billing envelopes or community newsletters.

- Your local newspaper might add your parade as an insert on an entertainment or activities page.

- Find a part-time PR volunteer. Try a college student studying PR or communications.

TV Coverage of Your Parade

If television is one of your goals, it's achievable but might take a few years—or it might be closer than you think!

Traditional television advertising is tough. For most local stations it will cost you $20,000 and up for a Saturday morning parade. This cost can be offset via commercials. Talk to your largest sponsor and see if they will pick up the tab by placing their own commercials into the coverage.

Stations have some licensing responsibilities to the community. They answer to the FCC, the Federal Communication Commission. It's the Title III of the Communications Act. Knowing this might help you sell coverage of your parade to the station.

If the parade is appealing to the majority of the community, getting coverage might be easier. Christmas parades of light and boat parades are examples. If you are the only parade in the area with the theme, you are more apt to get their TV coverage.

Keep in mind that, as you continue to make your parade more and more distinctive, the more likely your parade will be accepted for local TV coverage.

Remember, color TV wasn't mainstream until the early 60's. The late Bill Lofthouse, former president of Bent Parade Floats, noted in the 1992 *IFEA's Official Guide to Parades* that the way broadcasting of parades got started in the 50's was when a TV network executive said that if there was movement on the floats, they would give the parade more TV time. Keep this in mind when talking to a TV station. When you watch any parade on TV you will only see the most interesting and dynamic entries and not the whole parade.

Coverage might be done through your community's exclusive cable TV station. Or if you have computer knowledge, you might be able to air it on a live computer telecast.

For mainstream TV stations, develop three-minute broadcasts to show the network station you are interested in. Be sure to promote how unique and interesting your parade is. For editing help, ask a city cable TV employee with experience.

Facebook Advertising

I ran the following ad seven days before parade day in 2012. The theme was sports. I believe it got outstanding results. Each year of the two years I did this, our attendance soared. The ad featured a headline reading: **"Huge Arvada Parade Sat A.M."** with a picture of the U.S. flag. The text read: "Olympian & Torch, 17 Bands, Silhouettes, Pro Sport Mascots, Clowns. Ed Tomlinson, Chair." I targeted the 52,000 Arvadans on Facebook.

Sign Code Problems?

Many communities are not letting events have signs promoting their upcoming parade along the parade route. They view signs as eye clutter. To stay within the law, review Improve Your Atmosphere in Chapter 1.

Signs can be put on private property. Check your local community sign code.

Many communities will exclude your parade from the sign code if asked. It might take a year or two to get this done, but work toward it or request a grandfather clause.

Freedom of Speech

Parades are a magnet for protest groups, both pro- and anti-. Anything controversial is now a political issue. The issues change from year to year.

Form your policy on how to handle these issues now as sooner or later they will be troublesome.

Parades across the nation are disrupted by these groups. Often the war of words starts in the media months before the parade. It's not uncommon for protest groups to interrupt the parade. They love attention and you're providing captive spectators.

Each year they get more and more emboldened in their efforts to attract the media. In some cases, people get hurt and some get arrested. Often, a parade gets cancelled in progress.

Civil disturbance is a gray area. Breaking windows or causing damage is not.

Know in advance what your police jurisdiction position will be with each type of issue such as a blockade, crashing the parade and being generally disruptive.

Moreover, what happens when one or more of the spectators gets upset and involved? What if the spectators start a shouting match and it escalates?

One entry applicant told me his unit was so controversial and upsetting in an earlier parade that one of the spectators attacked him during the parade.

The police will often check with the city attorney, who will advise the city manager who advises city council, before giving you an insight.

When allowing entries that are potential safety issues to your spectators, be sure to let your local police department know beforehand. Not necessarily to check them out, but to be aware and be in the area, in the event of trouble.

Who Owns the Streets?

You do. That's generally what a parade permit represents. You may not own the sidewalks unless it's spelled out.

Private Parades

Freedom of speech doesn't apply here. This has been hammered out in many court issues.

City/Government

Yes, freedom of speech "might" apply. There seems to be different opinions on this. Most municipal parades, however, do restrict those entries.

Blended

Often the city will contribute some in-kind value or give cash as a sponsor. Like any other sponsor, the city can opt out if they don't like your position. However, both the city and your parade committee need each other.

One method used to distract entries is to charge a political fee for political entries. After all, the entries are getting the same benefit the other political entries are getting.

If worst comes to worst, and you lose the city as a sponsor or they make it a part of the parade permit process, you might bring a lawsuit on the constitutional "freedom of assembly" issue. This applies to Canadian parades as well.

A rule of thumb might be, if the city is picking up more than 50 percent of the cost of the parade, you probably need to respect the freedom of speech rules if they ask you to, but *only* if they are not picking up 50 percent of the costs of other venues in the community.

Start a Free Speech Zone

To avoid some conflicts, think about offering a free speech zone on a public area.

Lawsuits on private parades have generally favored the parade organizers. One in Boston ordered the outsiders to be at least two blocks behind the parade. Another judge, in Laguna Beach, California, ruled that the militia wasn't welcome in the private parade.

Committees, entries and spectators put a lot of time and energy into a parade. Others with a different agenda want to take your work and use it to their advantage, not only for free but also with your captive spectators.

Remember, they can always form their own parade.

Weather

Here is some sample language that other parade committees are using:

- The parade committee plans to proceed with the parade, rain or shine.

- Should inclement weather occur prior to the parade, parade officials will determine if it's sufficiently severe to cancel or delay the parade.

- Entries may decline to utilize their float or specialty unit when weather threatens to damage uniforms, props or instruments.

- We request that you make provisions for foul weather and we will not refund registration fees (because of inclement weather) if it is your decision to leave the parade.

Professional Looking Forms

In general your forms and other printed materials need to be easy to read and very professional looking. Go to **Appendix C** for details.

Improving Your Application

Please go to **Appendix D**

Release of Liabilities

Please go to **Appendix E**

Signatures

Please go to **Appendix F**

3. PARADE SPONSORS AND FUNDING

Determining Your Value 101

Most parades lose money, however, you can improve on that. And if your parade can just break even or do a bit better, you won't need to look for or be as dependent on funding. If you're making money, then you can fund your reserves and/or grow the parade.

To start, you should consider your parade as a business, but do so quietly. If you are overt about the business aspect of your parade, be sure you have the backing of your key people. Some will not support it looking like a business.

Put together a "business plan." Without one, it's harder to improve year by year. The parade must look good, be engaging and be a positive experience for the entries and spectators. Your business goal is quality. Quality parades outperform all the others.

Your Feedback

"Sponsorship is all about the sponsor, not about you. When you start worrying about the sponsors and what they are getting, you will be highly successful...Just remember 50% of sponsorship dollars is committed in the last quarter of the year (October/November/December) so don't start late."

Sylvia Allen CFEE
Holmdel, New Jersey
Author of "How to be Successful at Sponsorship Sales," "The Art of Negotiation" plus 20 webinars on sponsorships
President of Allen Consulting, Inc.

How Many Spectators?

Most committees do not have a good answer for how many attended. Often you get an exaggerated guess.

You could take an aerial picture of the parade route during the event to count your spectators. Count the number in a square inch and multiply from there.

Your Feedback

"An interesting study, titled 'Analytically Estimating Crowd Attendance at a Parade,' published by the School of Public Affairs of Arizona State University, attempted to figure out attendance at parades. The results were 'significant.' According to the study, results show 'promise, but with need for further investigation. Adding a research element on how people travel to and park at a parade may also lead to an advanced or different understanding of maximum crowd size. If methods to estimate attendance can be refined and universally accepted they will replace SWAG (scientific wild-ass guesses) and someday provide accurate attendance figures to plan, coordinate, budget, evaluate, and report on the success of parades,' the researchers wrote."

Vern Biaett, CFEE
School of Community Resources and Development, Arizona State University

An expanded discussion on this is located in the Resources Section in the back of this book.

You also could film the spectators along the parade route before it starts and again near the last unit for medium-size parades. Putting video cameras on non-paying entries such as a fire truck or a committee's golf cart can accomplish this.

Use a hand-held counter while watching one side of the parade route video. Click once for every ten people or so. Repeat the process on the other side of the street and combine.

Average the totals for the beginning and end of the parade videos for a more accurate count. This helps in pricing entries. If it's more than a 10 percent difference, the entries at the end of the parade are worth more money.

Estimate the number of spectators and the people participating in the parade, and consider the size of the venue that amount would fill. For example, if you take the hundreds of participants and the thousands of people watching, that will just about fill your local pro sports stadium or several of your high school football stadiums or school auditoriums.

Who are your spectators? Use this to focus the direction of the type of sponsors you are looking for.

This demographic information is what your better sponsors want to know. These facts make it easier for them to make a decision and it will give your parade more credibility.

Your Budget

Your Feedback

The Magic of Parades

"Parades are magical! They are magical whether they are nationally televised productions like the Rose Parade or Macy's Thanksgiving Day Parade, or whether are just community parades, which don't get exposure beyond the bounds of the community they are held in. These parades are magical for participants as well as for the people that turn out in droves to watch them. And they are magical for all ages. Children love them, adults love them and senior citizens love them. Watch the face of a child at a parade and see the smiles and the wonder. Or watch the face of a senior citizen—like I have—and see the excitement and the youthfulness it brings to their face.

"Parades are also magical for the community in which they are held. In my home town, Pasadena, about 300,000 people come from out-of-town each year to enjoy themselves and to stay, eat and shop in our community and in the communities surrounding it. Even in small towns, people get out and participate in the town's well being as a result of parades. Just as importantly, parades of all sizes play a tremendous role in defining and uniting their community. They instill pride in the residents and participants, and instill a favorable image of the community in the minds of visitors. Many a community's reputation has been made or fostered by the parades they sponsor and nurture.

"Sadly, municipal governments around the country have taken to overlooking the positive aspects of parades, many of which can be intangible. The officials in these communities have begun looking at parades either as nonessential events they can cut from their budgets or as a source of new revenue for the municipal coffers. My colleagues around the country tell me in anguish of the new financial charges they now have to pay for services that were gladly provided free of charge only a few years ago. Many of these charges threaten the very existence of the parade or other associated events that make the magic for the community. I understand the pressures facing municipal government officials around the country, but I urge them to think about the magic of parades and the many ways they enhance and enrich their communities. Parades are worth the effort and expense for all concerned! After all, how can you price magic?"

Mitch Dorger

Former CEO Pasadena Tournament of Roses Association
His Webinars include
"The Dirty Dozen of Poor Governance: Overcome These Common Mistakes to Improve Board Governance"
"Building a Constructive Board-Staff Partnership"
"The Role of the Board—Inside and Outside of the Board Room"

Formalize your parade budget on an Excel spreadsheet or handwritten. Excel works well here because your budget may be changing weekly. If you can't do it yourself, find someone who can and give them a title, such as Budget Chair.

Create one budget that is actual and another as your "vision budget." Pass out your vision budget to committee and civic members and keep the actual one for the executive committee. One way to tell the difference is to use black ink on the original spreadsheet and make the vision spreadsheet in color for quick identification, depending on what meeting you're attending.

Keep adjusting as you gain funding and expenses. Remember you're in a growth mode.

Your Feedback

"I like your idea of different colors for different budgets! I like to call the actual budget a 'working budget.' I use QuickBooks and can quickly export a report into Excel for these purposes. If someone doesn't have those capabilities, then the idea of a working/actual budget is a great suggestion. Also, the vision budget is something to look to as well. I would suggest keeping that a constant and not adjusting. This gives a good idea of where you hit or missed your mark on numbers. In the end, it's a good idea to combine the vision budget in one column, then the actual and then a variance column. At my company we keep that document rolling from year to year and just hide the columns for the years prior but they are a quick 'unhide' button away from being able to reference them. When we start the new year's budget, we always keep the previous year's 'vision' budget and actual budget in view along with the new year's 'vision' budget. We keep a difference column at this point, but the difference is between last year's actual and the new 'vision' budget amounts.

"As a parade grows, it's easy in Excel to add new line items (general ledger accounts) for both income and expenses. You may even take items that were lumped into areas and spread them out. When we do this, we add the new line item and keep the previous year's amounts in the account where they were first reported. This might show large variances from year to year. We always have aNotes" column where we would explain the variances. For example, you sold tickets one year and everything went to 'ticket sales.' Then you created different types of tickets--maybe you added a group ticket program or VIP ticket program. The first year you have these new programs, the comparison to the previous year would be zero. Just explain, ticket sales moved from one type to three in the notes column.

"In the 'next year' section, I agree...start right away while it's fresh. And yes, base your new budget on the outcome of what actually took place and always cushion a bit for the unexpected. As you grow the unexpected will continue to be there!"

Pam Sartory
Business Manager, Sunfest of Palm Beach County, Inc., Florida

Who Are the Sponsors?

Sponsors are as varied as parades, and can include government and local, regional or national businesses. In some cases a private individual or civic club can be found. Over the past three years, sponsors have been tougher to find and to keep due to the tough economy. However, many still know the value they get in supporting you.

Local businesses are hit all the time. But once they hear your vision and you can prove value, quite a few will sign up. Each year as your parade grows in popularity, count on more sponsors and more entry income.

Always speak to what's in it for them or speak in terms of their "benefit." Never discuss what you want or why you want it.

Consider how they operate. Government, regional and national business sponsors often work on a yearly budget, so try getting them lined up for next year, not next month. Once they are in, they often will participate automatically in the years to come.

One way to show a large prospective sponsor what you can do for them is to invite them to have a seat on next year's grandstand.

Look around further. Can you qualify for your state's Lottery Commission money for your advertising expenses? Does your state collect some kind of taxation for cultural groups that you can qualify for?

Sponsorship Levels

Naming your sponsorship levels should have a professional look. Yes, many use metal names (gold, silver) but here is my best guess as to the pecking order:

Start with Title Sponsor. Title sponsors get the naming rights. Then the order of categories is Presenting Sponsor, Associate Sponsor, Supporting Sponsor, Contributing Sponsor, Official Sponsor, Media Partner, Official Supplier and Donor. The word sponsor in the title is important to the giver.

Your parade should implement this professional approach even if you only need a few of the sponsor levels rather than putting them all under the same classification or simply as sponsor.

What's the Difference Between a Sponsor and a Donor?

A good rule of thumb is that donors give less than $500. Over that, they are sponsors. If that arbitrary figure doesn't work for you, pick your own number. Remember that not everyone should be treated equally.

Some parades spend $500 in actual sponsor expenses for a $250 donation. Donors are to be appreciated, but don't give away the farm. Put them on your website in a donor classification called "donors" or "friends of."

Medium-sized parades consider certain sponsorship criteria before accepting a sponsor. Does the sponsor's image support the purpose of your parade? Are they good corporate citizens? Will they be long-term sponsors? Do the sponsors understand what it takes to put on a parade and help you with that? An example would be including mention of your parade in their advertising.

Many parades find it's best to have sponsors for specific components of the parade. If you go this route always charge more than your actual cost..

Exclusive Sponsors?

A potential sponsor rarely wants or assumes they will be exclusive. When you pick up a newspaper and see one sponsor's full-page ad across from another competitor's full-page ad, you get the picture. If they insist on exclusivity, that's an extra asset value and commands more money. Thank you to the Bruce Erley Creative Strategies Group for this tip.

The Colorado Springs, Colorado Veterans Day parade, for example, charges 10 percent of its $30,000 costs for a sponsorship and gets ten sponsors, treating each one equally. When a sponsor wants to pay more, they turn them down so they don't need to worry about offering or supporting separate tiers. You can adopt this philosophy using any dollar amount.

What Do You Charge a Sponsor?

You first must inventory your exposure assets. This will be foreign to most parade committees and it's actually become big business and even an industry. Think about every little detail of benefit to the sponsor and list these assets. Take a scientific or analytical look.

You will get better at this as time goes on. For example, how many individual posters and handouts? Does the sponsor get its name on every page of your website? Its logo? On your stationery? Each of these assets has a definable dollar value to your sponsor.

As you gain a better understanding of the concept it's easier to sell it to yourself, the committee and the sponsors. So many committees will take sponsors with a $100 or $200 donation and treat them almost the same as the larger sponsors to show appreciation because they have never been fully introduced to this kind of detail using an appropriate microscope.

Each level of sponsorship must offer different amounts of exposure. Exposure is what sponsors want.

Some people make their living by professionally finding sponsors for your event. Some of these promoters have even earned professional designations within their industry. Hire a promoter on your behalf, but only if you're looking to raise tens of thousands of dollars.

Small parades probably have twenty-five to fifty "assets," medium parades grow up to one hundred or more and large parades can actually count five hundred or more.

How can that be? Here are some examples of assets.

- How many times is the sponsor's name mentioned via a microphone?
- How long is each commercial on your microphone? Fifteen seconds?
- Does the sponsor have the opportunity to speak to your crowd?

- A logo is worth more than just their name
- How many sponsor banners are you allowing? One, five?
- When speaking to any group of people do you mention the sponsor?
- When speaking to the media, is the sponsor's name mentioned?
- Do you offer exclusivity?
- Is there a multi-year renewal option?
- Does the sponsor get coverage on your promotional materials such as hats and T-shirts?
- If you are meeting with the media, are they invited to attend?
- Do you give their name and number to the media during the phone interview, their email inquiry or your press release?
- How dominant a presence in a printed program do they get?
- Do they get to be on your stationery?
- An ad on your website?
- How many flyers are you printing with their name on it?
- A link from your website?
- A video on your website?
- A free entry into the parade?
- Are they mentioned on your forms?
- Is their banner on the reviewing stand?

There are literally hundreds of these assets. Once you start listing your assets, you need to value them. Being on your website is worth 1.5 cents per view.

As mentioned, every asset can be translated and unequivocally substantiated into a quantifiable value. This value is known in advance and is part of the value total. The higher the total value, the higher level your sponsorship is.

If you are doing this on your own, think of a value for each asset that is credible to your committee. By doing it this way, you will be able to present it with confidence.

You must be able to show that they are getting twice the *value* of the funding they agree to. But not dollar for dollar that you spend. Some of these assets are tangible and others intangible.

Put these assets to paper, work it out as to what each parade classification gets charged. You will be proud of it once you can substantiate it. Also post it on your website. All parades should post each classification and what the sponsor gets in return. You need to be sure that they are no longer treated simply as a donation and never again equally unless everyone is paying the exact same amount.

Your sponsors will do the math much better than you will. Some will consider this as a donation unless you show them the difference. They will truly support you once they know that your offer has an articulated value. Some will even ask to move up to a higher level of sponsorship.

Others may ask if you can do something for them that isn't on the list. Maybe it's multiple placements in the parade. Maybe it's seating on the grandstand for their children. Say yes and add it to your list of assets next year. Or if it's tangible enough, it requires negotiation for more sponsorship money to cover it.

Floats and Inflatable Balloons

Be sure to collect more than your costs. Many parades supply the unit and then sell the entry as a package or even as a turnkey.

Servicing Your Sponsors

Once you have a sponsor you need to make good on your promises. Both before and during the event, you need to convey that you are performing the promises. You must review the list of promises and make sure you are delivering. Many people make some promise, take the money and forget about it or they assume someone will be fulfilling it or the client kind of knows. When you do this you are treating them as a donation and disrespectfully. When you do follow through, the clients' heads will turn as their sponsorship has never been treated with this much respect. This helps not only your relationship but future and larger sponsorships next year.

Some committees will have a pre-parade party, such as a barbeque for the sponsors, and can share this information with them and ask what else you can do for them this year or next. Often the Grand Marshal will be introduced to them at this time. Many sponsors won't come, but being recognized this rare way proves to them they are being treated not as a donor.

Fulfillment

Then you need to prove to the sponsor that you did each of these things. This is called fulfillment. It's done by sending them a sample or pictures of everything you did for them. This will become very sophisticated the larger the sponsor is. It might be done in a scrapbook format and videos. A lot of work? Yes, but once you have done it once, it gets easier.

Expert Advice on Sponsorship

This book is not designed to give you an in-depth look at how to identify and price each asset and get and fulfill sponsorships. Please look at the International Festivals and Events Association online book store for state of the art support in books and webinars. In addition, *Yours for the Asking* by Reynold Levy is available at Amazon and bookstores.

Governments

Cities and others might fund your parade, providing partial financial or in-kind support. In-kind support often includes police overtime, portable toilets, barricades and the street sweepers. Sometimes it's free park fees and electricity. Keep track of their value and make sure they get sponsorship credit for what they bring to your table. Treat them as you would any other sponsor; they deserve it. If you don't, sooner or later they will ask for reimbursement. More and more cities are asking parade officials to pay their costs. If yours isn't now, it will soon.

What's in it for the community leaders? Prestige and increasing community pride is often cited...plus revenue from sales tax within the community before and after the parade. Please review throughout this book, additional reasons.

Yet many city fathers don't have a grasp of what your parade brings to their table. Some even get complaints from businesses that your parade costs them money in lost business. They may even close down during the parade. This is a tradeoff for tens of thousands of parades and not unique to you. Often your parade was there before they were.

Keep track of which organizations, schools and clubs participate, help and support the parade. Canvas businesses along the parade route that benefit from the parade and ask for testimonials on what impact the parade has on them. A fast food chain might say it's their busiest day of the year.

You can create a mini-survey that asks some of the following.

- Did you close for the parade?
- Did you receive more exposure to your business?
- Did the parade help your business?
- Did you receive more walk-in traffic?

Plus include a place for writing in comments.

Keep a list of where you spend money on parade expenses. Small parades spend hundreds of dollars, medium parade budgets can reach $30 thousand and large ones in the hundreds of thousands.

This expense information is important for local officials and committee members to know and understand. In return you will get even more support or, at the least, maintain it.

Your Feedback

"Cities play a central role in ensuring events organizers and participants get the support, infrastructure and services necessary to assure that every parade/event is a success. Developing a relationship with your City partners creates a common framework within which events managers, City events staff, City services (such as Traffic Management and Emergency Services) as well as citizens can ensure the success of the event."

Delores MacAdam
City of Ottawa, Canada
Manager, Licensing, Programs, Special Events

Concessions

Not too many parades offer concessions as they have not been successful. But yours might be an exception. Below is a quick review.

Alcohol

This is your number one money maker.

Pepsi/Coke Stands

This is your second largest money-making entity. Many organizations are moving toward having their own Pepsi/Coke stands at the end of the parade. This means that no other vendor or unit can offer, for free or for sale, water, fountain drinks and colas. All sales go to your booth. Let other concessionaires know the rules in their applications. If you do this be sure to tell the entries in the staging letter you send them that it will be there.

Your Pepsi/Coke supplier might supply, set up and take down their stand for you. They can supply ice, storage, and on-site support to make sure you never run out of product. It's turnkey if you're large enough. After your first year, ask them if you qualify for sponsorship cash. This gives you cash up front regardless of the weather.

To sell this to the spectators, simply let them know beforehand and with signage that the proceeds are going toward paying for the parade.

Be forewarned: the Pepsi/Coke people might require you to buy their ice at twice the cost. You might also be getting more than you need if the weather doesn't support it, taking a large percentage of your profits.

Community Food Booths

This is the third largest money-making entity. You can optionally furnish the booth and let the local PTA's, civic groups and scouts run it. These groups are getting a single donation fee, per-hour fees or a percent of the net profits.

Your Entry Fees

Do you have enough income from the city or an adjoining festival to cover your costs? As your parade grows, new entries will contact you and funding will be easier to get. Especially during your civic club circuit, when you show how much value an entry or a sponsor gets. They spread the word to other family members and friends who might own a business.

With more money, you can provide an even better parade. Here are some ideas.

Entry fees alone rarely pay for a parade. Your fees should be according to the value the unit is getting. Think about putting the fees on a sliding scale.

In addition, take into consideration the outlay the unit is contributing to create the unit. If they are spending say $1,000 and you want $100 but they add enormous value, you might want to waive the fee.

Multiple Entry Fee Schedule

Consider publishing a fee schedule that changes over time. Let's say last year's fee is $100. So six months early, it's $75, four months early it's $100, two months early it's $125 and then it's $150. What is your actual entry fee? $150 or is it $100?

You should email last year's entries early to put this into place to forewarn them. Maybe also do so just before each price change.

Defining your rate structures increases funding. Multiple entry classifications are appropriate. Entries benefit differently in parades. Each should pay for the value they receive.

Does a mom and pop hamburger stand have the same value as a McDonald's franchise?

Classifications

The better defined your entries classifications the easier it is to determine their value. Many parades generalize, for instance, a nonprofit classification.

This allows your committee internal debate on specific types of entries. This will also help to solve or defend a lot of issues for you and helps to attract or detract those entries that you may or may not want.

- **Sixteen semi's?**

Limit the number of vehicles in any one unit. Many parades charge extra per vehicle after the first two or three. Most limit each unit to two vehicles. Some parades charge up to a $500 fee per vehicle as they don't want many motorized units. It all depends on what you want your parade to look like.

But always keep in mind what your spectators want: variety.

Here's an example. One parade had eighty cars in a car club. The following year, the same club had no problem paying $5 a car, after the first three; other parades charge $10 per vehicle. It gets back to what you want your parade to look like and your new vision.

Expensive cars are harder to get. They are concerned about damaging their clutches in a stop-and-go parade. Overcome this by putting them toward the front of the parade that moves forward constantly.

- **Two hundred people in one unit?**

Yes, it makes for a positive statement for the unit. However, the spectators get bored with row after row of people just walking. Many parades charge a dollar per person or marcher after forty to fifty people. Other parades simply limit the total number to forty or so.

We had an applicant who estimated six hundred people would be included. Luckily only forty or fifty showed up.

- **Individuals/families**

Some parades don't allow them; others charge $10 to $25 each. Individual classifications are sometimes expanded to family entries. None are allowed to market or promote anything.

- **Horses**

Many parades typically charge $5 per horse. This could be a trend. A few are at $15. What do you want your parade to look like?

- **Barricades**

A surcharge to entries of $25 is popping up.

- **Police overtime**

Haven't heard of this being charged yet, but an entry surcharge may be coming.

- **Portable toilets**

Not yet, but city fees are probably about to charge so you will need to add another surcharge. This could be based on the number of people in the unit.

A single surcharge of $25 can be instituted to cover portable toilets, barricades, etc. I think most entries will understand that.

- **Marching bands**

These are typically free but some bands are paying $300 to participate.

- **Nonprofits**

Typically free but some parades are charging $25. See Chapter 4 on eliminating nonprofits as a category.

- **Handouts**

The trend is growing and many parades are charging $100 for the right to do handouts over and above the entry fee because the unit is getting extra value. See also Sampling and Couponing later in this chapter.

- **Non-themed**

Charge a fee if the unit isn't themed. If this is your parade's purpose and vision, then this is another way to get there.

- **Fire department fee**

There are a few parades charging this fee because there are inspections required for floats and non-floats with gas generators. It's easy to justify and might be in your future. A few are charging $25.

- **Donations**

These can come from many sources. Use the scripts below to help encourage them. Don't forget to suggest being added to their will.

> Parade costs are underwritten by public contributions and we ask that you send your contributions with your application.
>
> This event is funded by community donations.
>
> Pass the hat along the parade route. Keep security in mind.
>
> We are unable to participate but would like to help by making a donation and/or sponsoring a float.
>
> Put payment information in your marketing using a layout that has a coupon border.

- **Licensing**

For large parades this can be a great revenue source. The Collegiate Licensing Company website or the Rose Bowl Parade and others will have some insights on how to do this. They include forms and commission percentages.

Your Feedback

> "My recommendations would be parade 'themed' tee shirts, noise makers, seat cushions, novelties, etc. We have a third party vendor that we have a contract with for a flat fee. He sells low cost items at our events that primarily appeal to children. This could include Mylar balloons, glow necklaces and assorted glow items, etc. Concessions such as cotton candy might work as well."
>
> **Bridget Sherrill** CFEE
> VP of Merchandising Kentucky Derby Festival
> Author of "Successful Event Merchandising"
> Webinar, "Finding the Balance that Best Fits Your Event"

- **Commercial entries**

Send them a compelling message via post card, phone call or email that speaks to what exposure they get for being in the parade. You should get a 2 to 4 percent response if it's working. Carry the message in a letter format around with you during the year and leave copies wherever you shop. You can find through many city websites a list of the largest businesses in your area.

- **The sticky issue of politicians**

If there is one category of entry that may cause headaches, it's politicians. They are dignitaries in many arenas but not here. Review again what the purpose and vision of your parade is. Political entries should in effect be taken off the pedestal and treated like all of your other entries. Don't lump all the different types of political entries together or call them a dignitary classification anymore. Each type of political unit has different values.

Most of you are probably letting political entries in for free or maybe charging up to $50. Some committees charge huge fees to discourage them. A few don't let political entries in at all due to the hassles they bring to the committee.

If you're a private or a blended parade, then are they riding free? If you let them in for free, do you then need to let all other government classifications in for free?

Please note that whatever fee structure you decide on, some say it should be uniform. If you charge one government group one rate and another a different rate they will suggest the lower rate for parity. Others think that different political groups get different value.

We tried a series of fees depending on the number of their constituents. Governors would pay the most and a council member who represented one seventh of the city would pay the least. It seems fair to me.

You will hear that your political unit fees should not be higher than a commercial unit fee. Political unit fees should actually be higher. Businesses have other ways of advertising and have a twenty-four-hour lighted building marquee to support them. This is a one-time event for political units. Business is ongoing and has many other advertising options than short-term candidates or elected officials do.

Many might say that we have to let political units in for free because you can't change tradition. Others will say they will get angry or hurt us politically if we start charging them.

Your Feedback

"Every festival or event must engage in political activities and tactics necessary to remain viable in a turbulent governmental and societal environment. Every community is different but it is still necessary for an event to play politics as this can have a positive (or negative) effect on your revenue, attendance, sponsorship, property, opportunities and respect."

Chip Baker, CFEE
Chattanooga, Tennessee
Executive Director Riverbend Festival
Author of "How Playing Politics Can Pay Off," and other articles

Read on and put together your own position paper as to why this is now of value to them and what your parade expenses are. They will be surprised or shocked at what it costs to put on the parade, that it loses money, and they will be much more open to the idea of having to pay to get in.

Ask them if they want you to start charging the charities and civic clubs instead of them.

Make changes all at once. Take the heat this year and then it will be accepted each year thereafter as customary. If you dribble it in, then you get political heat each year.

It's tough enough running a parade without this kind of heat. Besides, it's supposed to be fun, isn't it? Political discussions pitting you or others against each other are perhaps the most controversial issue in running a parade.

When you do make changes, announce them months or a year in advance. Be sure to email or call everyone with the new rules and your justification as early as you can.

Politicians allowed on the microphone can be charged by the seconds. Never give them the microphone. You must hold it or lose control.

Political entry fees range up to $550 if allowed in at all.

You bring a turnkey opportunity. They show up, say hi and wave to hundreds or thousands of their constituents. All this is for free, a good use of their time—and at your expense. For them, this is branding and adding value to the politician via name recognition and top of mind consciousness.

Once you institute a fee system for politicians, it will become tradition and create a long-term income stream. See also ballot issues, below.

- **Political candidates running for office**

These can include your city council, county, township and borough commissioners, fire boards, special district boards, park boards, school boards, sheriffs, county assessors, county surveyors, county coroner, state and U.S. representatives, and senators and governors.

The candidates in your parade cannot get this kind of belly-to-belly, eye to eye, exposure in any other medium. The larger the number of spectators, the more value being in the parade is to the candidate.

Think about what it costs for a town hall meeting, mailings, PR people, manpower, rental facilities, handouts and media. How many come to their event, a few dozen, a hundred, a thousand—or two?

How much exposure do they get and what does it cost to run a business card size ad in your local newspaper—a few hundred dollars? No advertisement is as effective as *your* "captive spectators."

The cost of each thirty-second radio ad starts at $400. A thirty-second cable ad in your area might run a thousand or two. A TV ad can run over ten grand.

Handbill distribution often runs ten cents a house plus printing and editing.

Think of the time the candidate would spend knocking on doors as compared to being in front of parade spectators.

Elections can be won or lost on a few dozen votes. Don't minimize or under-value these entries in your parade.

What is the value of the spectators seeing another spectator shouting good things to the candidate? The nearby spectators are influenced favorably to this.

They get a free announcement at your reviewing stand. And, if you have more than one reviewing stand, the value continues to rise.

Edit and add this list of benefits to your website application form, to show how much value they are getting.

Don't underestimate or discount the value your parade brings to their table. Their campaign committee can't afford not to do it even if the money is from the candidate.

- **How much to charge political candidates?**

Determine the number of spectators at your parade. After trying several different price points over the years we determined one cent per spectator. This assumes the spectators are generally 75 percent local. Remember, the more the candidates complain, the more they recognize the value of your parade. Otherwise they can simply opt out. If you find they all opt out or a large percentage of them do, next year reduce your fee because the market has spoken to you.

- **Elected officials—office holder**

Elected officials have a different dollar value compared to a political candidate. They might be worth one-half cent per spectator.

Remember you have costs. Often parade committees furnish convertibles from local car dealerships and signage. My costs were over $600 for the signs, at $20 each for both sides of the car years ago.

If they are up for re-election, they often will pay twice. They may choose to ride as an elected official without Vote for Me signage and then again in their own political candidate unit.

This exposure gives the elected official additional name recognition for their next election or political future. What is that value that you bring to their table?

If you get resistance on raising the fee, remind them that city hall or the entity they are running for creates or raises fees on housing, parks, permits or water for a better income stream. You're doing the same thing here.

Of course you would not charge those who give you in-kind services or cash donations. However, this gives you further evidence of the value you bring to them as a sponsor. Sometimes your value will total more than the in-kind value they bring to the table. This knowledge could help in increasing your in-kind sponsorship revenue from those entities.

- **Ballot issues**

Charge them the same rate as other political entries. Letting them in for free, as long as both sides are represented, might create a ruse. Often only one side is outwardly interested in the parade. A fake unit will be entered on behalf of the opposing point of view, in order to get in for free.

- **Politics and your spectators**

Don't take this classification lightly. This can be difficult to handle and can become violent. Every year protestors get more and more emboldened. They love captive audiences and you're delivering them. Some protesting entries will even stop the parade or, worse, disband it. Their goal is not to inform the spectators but to get media attention before, during and after the parade.

Use private security if you need to. Get buy-in from the police otherwise the cops will dislike you using them. Balance this with the knowledge that you are the committee and it's your responsibility to protect your spectators, the integrity of your parade and your entries.

Every year there is some new issue that is hot. It can be gay, militia, Columbus, abortion, war, immigration, health care, capitalism and guns. They will protest it's "freedom of speech." Most parades, city and private, simply don't allow them in. Determine your values and defend your position.

- **Political parties**

If they pay the fee, they are in. But many parades let them double up by putting all of their candidates or issues in their unit. Don't allow doubling up. They cannot support in any way something other than their party. No candidates, office holders or issues unless fees are paid for each one. Can you imagine what the reaction would be if a commercial unit added in several other commercial entries to theirs to bypass the fee?

- **Paid parking**

Is there some private property that has the right location supporting your needs? Sometimes a business will close for the day just to rent out its parking lot. Something to consider.

- **Special requests?**

Everybody wants to be in the front of the parade. Some have special needs. Try charging a $25 fee for being in the first half and $50 for being in the first quarter of the parade and see what happens. Your free entries might even pony up for this.

Try this Demonstration—Here is a suggestion for handling requests to be in the first section of the parade line-up.

Take a piece of paper and say to the person or group that wants to be in the front of the parade that "this represents all of our parade entries." Tear off about 15 percent of the sheet. Comment—with a smile—that the politicians want to be in the front, as they have better things to do with their time. Tear off another section. "This represents the children in the parade. They need to be up front as they get bored and have to go to the bathroom." Tear off another section; "this represents the civic clubs. They have to be up front in order to man the community booths at the fair." Tear off another piece. "This represents the bands that need to get to a field performance or practice somewhere." Tear off another section. “This represents the sport teams that need to get to the game.” Tear off another piece.” This represents the seniors who need to get out of the sun.” Now all you have left is the one piece that represents the horses.

This demonstration helps show that everybody has a legitimate reason to be up front. Most of the time, you will create a good connection with your audience. If you are doing a presentation, use this demonstration at the beginning or end of your discussion—whenever the most people are there to see it.

- **Sampling**

If a unit wants to work the parade route and give free samples, they must pay your sampling fee. If they just want to work the sidelines and not be in the parade, they should pay your entry fee as well. The sampling fee might be 15 cents per dollar value of the sample. This is different than using coupons. Your spectators are actually getting the opportunity to test the products on the spot, which is why it has extra value.

- **Couponing**

Compared to sampling, couponing is very direct-marketing driven.

Example: One Dairy Queen outside the city passes out many coupons and receives enormous return on them. This is verified as they must go to that particular DQ site to redeem. The franchise knows exactly what kind of response they are getting from your parade. You can’t get the same income as sampling but you can negotiate a figure depending on the value of the coupon and the number of spectators. Charge those 3 percent each plus an entry fee.

- **Golf carts**

Allowing a banner on a golf cart is another value that your sponsor can receive. Remember, a golf cart will be seen by a lot more people than a banner that is stationary. You may have a major sponsor and someone wants to give you $100 for signage on a golf cart. Make sure the price is not unfair to your larger sponsors.

- **Emcees**

To raise money, offer to local businesses the emcee position. You could charge them anywhere from $50 to $5,000 each, depending on attendance and media coverage. Allow them on air three times at fifteen seconds each, to promote their business, but pick quality ones, as they represent you and your committee.

- **Volunteers**

Some parades actually charge the volunteers to be involved. If you do, then you know that you’re a well-received parade. Surprised? Cheyenne Frontier Days does it very well. Think of it as a club with dues or a membership fee.

They may charge $25 or $50 to cover the costs of the volunteers and an after dinner party or luncheon, commonly called a benefit package. The number of parade volunteers can add up to over four hundred.

As a side note, the events at the Indy 500 utilize around 6,500 volunteers.

- **In-kind**

Lots of people donate items and time to your parade. Treat them with respect, give them some credit, but as a rule, unless it's worth is over $500, it's a donation.

Let in for free those entities that give you in-kind benefits. Keep track of how much value you give them and compare it to how much in-kind value you're getting. At some point you might find that having fifteen free city entries is above the in-kind value you're receiving. You don't need to charge them, but you do need to let them know what they are getting to forestall any new city reimbursement costs to you.

- **Water bills marketing**

Can you insert a free advertisement or comment into your community's water bills a month or two before your parade? You could offer this to sponsors. You may not be able to put the sponsor's logo in the message but you might name them as the Presenting or Title Sponsor.

Imagine the value of this to your sponsor. A direct mail piece would cost roughly 50 cents for a post card and about a $1 for an envelope mailing. Multiply this times the number of water meters and you get the picture. A rule of thumb on the number of water meters might be one-third of your population total.

Ask to be inserted into your community's online or mailed newsletter.

- **Late fees**

Some parades don't allow late entries, others charge 50 percent to 100 percent of the entry fee. Remember, if they are calling you after the deadline, they want in and will pay whatever you decide in almost all cases.

- **VIP tent**

Find a sponsor who needs political contacts to pick up this tab.

It requires fencing and other minor security. The food and beverages are usually supplied free, via local restaurants.

- **Bleachers**

Charge $5 to $17 per person for the best seats? Or ask businesses to put them up for the general public, enhancing your parade and saving you money.

Bleachers are tough to make money on as the cost per seat often is $5 to break even. If you can have stadium seating, this is a huge profit center.

- **Website**

Any time someone clicks on your website and sees a sponsor's logo it's worth a penny and a half. That's the industry standard. Links are worth more. It's even worth more if they click through.

- **Programs**

Get a marketing agency to handle programs with you getting a percentage of the gross. They go out and sell the ads while you supply and control the content. Usually the business advertiser gets a couple dozen programs each to hand out, two weeks before the parade. The balance of the programs are distributed as a local paper insert or handed out along the parade route before the parade starts.

If your local paper is doing this at no cost to you, but receiving the revenue it's time to ask for a percentage. What are they charging? Sometimes it's $1,200 a page. If you can't get a percentage, then negotiate for column inches in the paper and the dates you want.

Be aware, individuals selling the ads may try and take ownership of the program content. This can include contacting your best sponsors for money and dictating other specifics to you.

- **Free entries**

Over half of your entries are probably free. It's almost impossible to charge scout groups and schools to be in a community parade. If your parade needs culling, start charging some basic fees, like $25, and they will slowly be eliminated.

- **Miscellaneous**

Do you have a festival that pays for the parade?

Does your parade bring more activity to your festival? Doesn't this create value that you should be compensated or given credit for?

Does your parade let everyone in for free? Many of these parades lack an audience because every Tom, Dick and Harry is in it, and is not interesting unless the rules are stringent.

How much dollar value is it for the ones leading the parade if it's not a sponsor?

Charge a $50 clean-up fee for those passing things out.

You may find opportunities to rent out to other clubs or organizations whatever you use in the parade, year after year.

Some Additional Thoughts

Are you feeling underpriced? You will get better at pricing over time. You need this as your costs are going up each year. Invoke as many changes in one year as you can get away with. Dragging out this debate over several years will be tough. You will be having the same difficult, time-consuming discussions over and over again.

Do you have suggestions or ideas? Send me your thoughts on the Community Parades Facebook page.

4. PARADE ENTRIES

Quality entries look for well-run events.

Valerie Lagauskas
Philadelphia, Pennsylvania
Formerly with the Macy's Thanksgiving Day Parade
Editor, 1992 IFEA's Official Guide to Parades
Founder/President, Synergistic Concepts, Inc.

Whole books could be written on parade entries alone. Parade committees may find this area the most challenging, but also the most exciting. Here are some of the issues that come up.

Reclassify or Eliminate Nonprofits?

Consider deleting the nonprofit category. So many entries that are not nonprofits use this title for free entry into the parade.

Otherwise, go to their website to see if they qualify. Or add to your parade rules that they submit a copy of their 501(c)(3) designations. This will truly give you an honest picture.

Rules Are Not Guidelines

Guidelines are more vague. The purpose of parade rules (**Appendix H**) is for the safest possible parade experience for the spectators and the entries. Rules are usually added because of some experience you had. Rules are not only to prevent lawsuits, but to be able to defend yourself in court with them.

Throughout this book, there are suggestions for rules. There are over three hundred additional thoughts used by other parades that might reduce your problems or risks in **Appendix H** of this book.

They include Entry Rules, Vehicle Rules, During the Parade Rules, Marchers Rules, Signage Rules, Band Rules, Performing Rules, Music Rules, Political Issue Rules, Distribution Rules, Inflatable Rules, Vendors, Staging Rules, Float Rules, Insurance Rules, Walkers/Contingent, Stewards/Monitors/Outwalkers Rules, Staging Marshals/Wranglers/Route Marshals Rules, Animals Rules, and Equestrian Rules.

Writing Your Rules

Shall and will mean the same as must? Do a word search in your rules. If you find "shall" and "must," try to be more specific. Here are some examples:

- Reserves the right to refuse...
- Final decision on type of entry is with the...
- Agrees to abide by...
- Signature required...
- Must approve all entries...
- Failure to follow...
- Except sponsors' clowns, bands, military units, scouts and students.

Application Deadlines

Don't have one? Do you let them call at the last minute? That's great, but as you grow, new demands and problems will appear.

To maintain a polished parade, create deadlines. Late-comers can be added but they won't understand last minute impacts on staging, the emcees or the scripts.

Should Your Volunteers Be in the Parade?

There is good debate on both sides. For some it's tradition, for others it's to show appreciation for all of their work.

Expanding the Number of Grand Marshals

Grand marshals are usually special individuals from the community. Look for opportunities in which you can honor a dozen or more people.

Just a thought, how many Medal of Honor winners do you have in your state?

How politically smart might it be in naming those leaders in your community from before 1970? Or local business icons, defined as being in business for at least, say, forty years? Would this add value to your parade? Does this create more credibility, support and sponsorship? Aren't they deserving and wouldn't they like to be recognized in this way? Think of the impact on the dozens of people selected and their friends and families rather than just one.

When we made the elder community leaders grand marshals, they loved it and so did the spectators. Everyone got to see people they had not seen in years. We put these men and women on one float, and they loved chatting before and during the parade about days gone by. Then they decided to have lunch together after the parade. How special, memorable and appropriate?

Our experience: one year, three citizens at age 90 or more were honored in this way. Originally we thought there would be twenty to twenty-five who might be over the age of 90. We discovered it was nearly two hundred! So we sent nice certificates to the assisted living homes and asked the activity director to pass them out. There was instructions that if they would like to be in the parade to let us know. Although no one called, we also contacted people living at home and got some attendees that way.

Announce early who your grand marshal recipients are for next year. This allows the new grand marshals and their families to delight in it all year long.

Next year we may offer the grand marshal honor to the "largest" employers in the community. How to define this? Does it mean schools, government offices and local grocery store chains? How about a business that has offices here but has hundreds of employees outside the city?

Your Feedback

> "We have had Jimmy Carter, astronauts, and many, many others as grand marshals. Last year it was Barbra Eden from the TV series I Dream of Jeannie. It's because of the enthusiasm of the committee that gets them there."
>
> **Carolyn Crayton** CFEE
> Macon, Georgia
> Cherry Blossom Festival

Dignitaries

These are the ones *you* decide on. They are not politicians. They are the Miss Xxx of your city or state, a local hero, a Man or Woman of the Year and the grand marshal(s). They are true dignitaries. Review your dignitary list and see if they still are appropriate. Some might be a business and don't qualify. Let them know months beforehand that the rules were change. We found that the few who were removed never complained as they recognized they didn't fit the definition.

No-Show Celebrities

Celebrities add credibility and interest to your parade. Normally celebrities want money and, if paid, they usually show up. Make sure you have an understanding about the agreement, for example, how long and what is expected of them, or you might be very disappointed.

If you do get them for free, you also must take the risk that they are no-shows or stay a far shorter time than you want. To minimize this risk, make them honorary chairs or honorary grand marshals, says Larry Lawyer, past president of Denver's St. Patrick's Day Parade. Let them know how large your audience will be. Try finding a local celebrity and ask him or her to chair your celebrity committee. Chances are your celebrity will invite other celebrities. It's likely all of them will show up.

Ask your major sports mascots to attend.

Contact your local talent agencies. They usually handle the contacts.

Is Cirque du Soleil coming to a town near you during your parade? They have a community outreach program and you might get lucky. Check it out and contact their PR department using some of the same language they used in their outreach. If they like what you write, they might forward it on to the right person. It also gives you more credibility going through these protocol channels as compared to contacting any national or international entity. We were partly successful here. In the end they decided a 9 a.m. parade would require them to get up at 4 a.m. as it takes three hours for makeup. They did show up at the festival later, however, and did face painting.

Thoughts on Elected Officials

Denver's St Patrick's Day Parade, a private parade, charged $550 for each elected official. They have over one hundred thousand spectators, many of whom are from out of the city. There also is TV coverage.

Our local parade used to offer free invitations to a few local officials and eventually expanded the invitation to all of them. This included governors, state reps, county commissioners, school boards, park, recreation and fire boards. They loved being a part of the parade.

The convertibles they ride in are free from dealerships, but it takes man-hours to find and coordinate them.

Nothing is ever simple. Here's an example. Once in a while some of the politicians would not like the car they were to ride in and requested another one on the spot. In one case, the donor of the private convertible wouldn't let certain people ride in it.

One year, a senator's staff member called the day before parade day and said it's customary to let her senator in. No problem, we said, but the day before means we scurry to get the signage done on the spot, change all of the emcee's books and reset the line-up! Shortly thereafter we added a deadline.

Do your spectators *want* politicians? Sure it's enjoyable for some to see these people, but the officials get much more out of it than your spectators do. They get branding, increased name identification for the next election even if it is a couple of years away. They get to see and wave at many friends who are or will be supporters.

Group your politicians on floats that consist of flat beds with straw bales and individual signage. This may not go over well with them, however. You will learn that this entity doesn't like that entity and can't be on the same float, or sometimes even the float itself is "demeaning." Remember these are the same people who are paying nothing for a parade that cost you hundreds or thousands of dollars to put on.

The best solution is to ask them to walk the parade route. As mentioned earlier, we can take an example from the U.S. president. When he gets out of his car to walk alongside it, everyone is thrilled. Put the convertible in the parade for signage and as backup. But engaging directly with the spectators makes a far better parade for the spectators *and* the politician than just driving by. But they must keep up with their unit. Beware, they often will slow down your parade.

If you do have politicians riding in separate cars, be prepared for requests to be in the front of the parade. This is because of tradition or they don't want to wait around for their unit to move or they have to be someplace else shortly thereafter. Instead, sprinkle them throughout the parade. It gives them singular exposure and breaks up the monotony for the spectators.

In your letter to the politicians, explain the advantages of your new rules. When they are prepared, they won't book appointments the same day. If they are very busy, your staging letter will explain how they can show up closer to the time their unit moves during the parade. If they don't come at all, it's their loss. You're supplying the captive and attentive spectators, so you make the rules.

23 Marching Band Tips

1. Have you noticed that every student who plays an instrument wants to be in a parade? To help you keep this in the right perspective, most high school bands work on concert and field presentations. Not marching. If they do march, they have to practice and that takes away from these main areas of interest.

2. Remember, the band directors need to be flattered throughout the process. You want them to come because they want to, not because they have to. Some bands that are made to come may only march and not play.

3. Ask or demand that the band play X times along the parade route. Some will only play in front of the reviewing stand. They thrive on cash awards, large trophies and being judged. They are the most professional group in your parade. They operate at the same level as the military. It will be the most trained private group in your parade. Don't take them lightly.

4. Every spectator wants to hear the bands. They are America's favorite units in any parade. They dramatically improve your parade, so make them your number one priority. Because someone said no in the past doesn't mean it can't be done now. Positions and attitudes change and new management has different views.

5. Small- to medium-sized parades across America have zero to three marching bands in them. It often depends on the time of year.

6. Late summer and fall parades are a popular time for public school marching bands.

7. Why would bands or marching bands want to join your parade? Do they need the exposure or simply like the idea of being in a parade? Sometimes the reason is payback to the community that has supported them.

8. Ask around. Small groups get together for their own amusement.

9. Offer a large cash grand prize to attract them. An East Coast parade pays the bands $2,000 each with a first place prize of $4,000 to attract them.

10. Make sure you have expert judging to attract bands.

11. Email your high school band directors for ideas and direction.

12. Get names, leave cards or brochures on the bulletin boards at local music stores.

13. Go online to see what surfaces in your area.

14. Go to hotels and see what lists they have assembled that they choose from.

15. Contact your country clubs and inquire whom you might invite.

16. Look at a year's worth of back issues of newspaper entertainment sections at your library to learn which bands are playing where and when.

17. With budgets so tight, offer to reimburse them for transportation. School buses might run $125 plus 75 cents a mile. Large schools might need three buses and an equipment truck.

18. Email talent agencies. They need reasons to support their clientele.

19. Email your local colleges and high school music teachers for leads.

20. Military bands might attend if asked in advance. The closer they are to you, the better. You must offer to pay their transportation costs and never charge them an entry fee. Lunch, overnight lodging or air transport is appropriate if they come a long distance. Meals are usually mandatory, but occasionally transportation costs won't be required. The military fields a variety of musical units, and on the application form you can select "musical units" for a traditional marching band. Download the Request for Armed Forces Participation in Public Events (Non Aviation) form.

21. Invite brass bands. Drum and Bugle Corps (usually from May to August) might be available. See if there are community bands. Or start your own band by offering it to the community. Sure it takes work but everybody wins.

22. Contact the Shriners, Salvation Army, Scottish bagpipes, drum corps, tuba and clown bands.

23. Check your state's bandmasters and music education associations. They might need and sanction a high school marching band competition. These kinds of competitions are much in demand.

We paid $2,000 for an expert to set up a competition. We went from ten bands to seventeen the first year. Ten others dropped out the week before the parade because it fell on one of three ACT test dates. The band students next year will be asked early to pick a different date. We expect even more in the future at only a cost of a $500 yearly rate to the organizer.

Few bands can travel large or overnight distances to compete, so bring the competition to them. This can be a huge opportunity for your community, your spectators and your parade, but more importantly to the students.

High school bands need to enter a competition and use professional high tech parade videos that use booms to capture footwork and formations. These videos are sent to Macy's, Tournament of Roses, London, and presidential inaugurations for invitations.

At the reviewing stand, add a quiet zone of one hundred and fifty feet in each direction in the judging area so no other entries or emcees interfere.

Keep chalk and candy out of the quiet zone as they reduce the professionalism of the footwork videos.

Your Feedback

"At our community parade, in order to get a lot of bands to participate we have a competitive band contest as part of the day's event. We have a field competition, as well as a parade marching band competition.

"We involve the local community by having the local school band director to take on the responsibility of planning and implementing the "Band Day" as part of our parade. Our festival office works with the band director to get the schools addresses and director names so we can prepare the letters of invitation that are mailed to each school with the rules/guidelines for the festival parade and competition.

"They attend our parade committee meetings and report each meeting on their progress. They also involve the local parent band booster club to work the concessions that day at their field competition as a fund raiser for the band. They feed them hamburgers/hot dogs or whatever the parent band booster club decides to cook that particular year.

"There are cash prizes and trophies given to winners to entice them for first, second and third place finishes.

"We typically have about 25 bands from the South Central and Southern part of Oklahoma that compete.

"The event has grown so much that our parade now goes for 1½ hours in time frame with approximately an average of 90 parade entries, including floats, vehicles, walkers and bands.

"This past year we decided to limit entry into the parade to the first 10 bands to enter in order to cut the length of the parade time. Seems to have worked well for us."

Sheilla Brashier CFEE
Ada, Oklahoma
Director, Chickasaw Foundation, Special Services Department

How to Get New Commercial Entries

Go to your library, chamber of commerce, online and city hall. There are business lists of all local, county, regional and state businesses by size and types. Email them or their PR department. They will usually respond or forward your email to the correct department. Make sure it's well edited. Be brief but give an overview and be sure to say what's in it for them.

Sometimes you will need to book the entries well in advance. For example, the Oscar Meyer Weiner Mobile requires six months in advance. Many military units now only book via their websites. Their list of units (assets) is located there for you to choose from.

Attend parades in your state and watch other parades online or televised. Make a list of the entries you would like for your parade. If you are attending the actual parade, chat with the unit in the staging area or simply hand them a brochure, letter or card that includes an invitation.

Your Feedback

"Every day your local Chamber of Commerce, government business registration division, and a phone book company receive leads on new businesses in your area. Partner with these agencies and be the first in your community to extend the welcome wagon to these newcomers! Let them know about your event, discover what they have to offer, and work together to find a marketing or sponsorship strategy that is win-win. They're excited, they're hungry and they'll be incredibly appreciative that you took the time to help nurture their endeavors and introduce them to your audiences, volunteers and other sponsors."

Stephanie Donoho CFEE
Hilo, Hawaii
Tourism Specialist, Department of Research and Development, County of Hawaii

How to Get More Floats

Floats are interesting entries and are second only to marching bands. They create emotional reactions from the spectators. However, they are time consuming and can be expensive to build. The challenge for community parades is providing enough support. Many organizations and businesses, even if they had the money, don't have the volunteers to build one nor can they spare the employees the day of your parade. The big parades offer to build it for them. Then the families of their managers or employees get to work the entry.

But we know that spectators want floats and a larger variety of floats. Bill Lofthouse, past president of Bent Parade Floats, once wrote in the 1992 *IFEA Official Guide to Parades* to not let the large national parades define you. When you articulate the purpose of your parade, you will educate your community and redirect their thinking toward your vision.

Bill also said budgets generally dictate the size and scope of the float. A guideline to keep in mind when developing a float is, "It's not the amount of your budget that counts, but the concept you come up with to fit within that budget." Hire it done by a float builder. Contact art departments at schools, playhouses, and cultural centers to inquire if some of the staff would do this.

Your goal is to find businesses or clubs to build them. Encourage them and fully appreciate them. In some cases you might even donate some money for materials.

Help your entries learn how to be efficient both with volunteers' time and expense.

Assign a float chairperson. The task will be to learn ways to decorate floats, flatbeds and pickup trucks. They can learn how to make them cheap, easy and effective to support your entries via your website. Again, the large national parade websites are a good place to get additional information and ideas. They have links to all kinds of supporting information.

The extra-wide mobile and modular homes going down the highway have trailer frames you might be able to use. Some are 11.5 feet by 32 feet long, others are 53 feet and longer. Get some half-inch plywood from your local lumber store for a deck and you're on your way. These frames can easily be pulled by a small farm tractor or typical car or truck using a standard hitch. Dealers keep these trailers for a few months and then return them to the manufacturing plant. Reserve a trailer and in return put their banner on the float. These are great low-rise trailers for any parade.

One method to get more floats is to simply offer a sponsor a free entry if they meet certain guidelines. Example: If they spend over $1,000 on an entry, they get in for free. Or if it takes more than fifty or one hundred man hours to complete. The idea here is if they make a huge contribution to your parade, you might not want to charge them.

Offer schools money to come up with school floats for competition. To keep fortunate schools and less fortunate ones equal, limit the amount of money they can spend on each float. Go to the schools and ask which business now supports them in some way. Contact that business and see if they will be their sponsor. You must make it as easy for the entry as you can. This is one entry that needs your total support to make it almost turnkey for the decision makers.

Here are ideas. The Olympics come every two years. Why not become the Official Summer or Winter Olympic Parade in your state or at least get an entry? Or, is the Ringling Bros. and Barnum & Bailey Circus in town during your parade? They might want to get involved in yours to boost attention. Are there other national or international groups that are in town and might show up?

Novelty

Consider things like tricked-out baby stroller competitions, Teddy Bear parades and synchronized library cart groups. This includes promotional entries like the Pillsbury Dough Boy. These add extra value to your parade and add a nice break to the regular entries. You also can stage these novelties on their own, and not necessarily hold them on a street.

Inflatable Balloons

These are eye-catching and loved by the spectators. Like the floats, they have come to expect balloons in parades as they recall the Macy's Thanksgiving Day parade.

Having balloons in your parade will meet your spectators' expectations. They bring out the child in each of us. They will definitely improve your parade, its credibility and its value.

There are several types of inflatables. The industry names are Cold Air, Sealed, Air Tight, Helium, In Costume and Dynamic. The Dynamics are the stationary fabric tubes you see waving via an air pump located in the base. Keep in mind that, along the parade route, some traffic signals actually can be rotated. Power lines can be addressed in several ways, as discussed below.

Many corporate businesses have inflatables, especially the franchises and chains. When requesting them for your parade, be aware that local management may not even know corporate has them or else they have never thought about ordering one. These local chains will need to reserve it and pay a fee for it.

One thing to consider: helium balloons are more difficult to work with after about 11 a.m. The temperature and wind adversely affect them. Alternatively, most cold air balloons work all day long. In addition, I understand that the government has taken most of the helium and it's now rationed to the private sector. The cost has tripled. So a Macy-style balloon would cost $2,000 just for the helium.

Renting these balloons can be challenging, but worth taking the extra effort. Meet with any local manufacturers and they will help you if you appear credible. If you ask, they may even email your link to their past customers to give them more exposure.

Find a chairperson to research inflatables online in your area and state. Sometimes they are available for rent and the business can put its advertising on it. You will likely find a lot of stationary inflatables. You or your chair will need to meet with these companies, look through their inventory and suggest to them that the inflatable could be put on a flatbed. It will be novel to them. The inflatables often rent for $300 or so. Small, Macy's-style helium balloons start at $3,000 to purchase. You also might get a company to buy a short one that would go under power lines and use it in several parades each year. Try to get them to use it in your parade first.

Offer free entry into your parade if they have one. Make sure you set the right guidelines to qualify.

Your Feedback

> "Air-inflated WalkAround costumes are a very cost effective way to add some excitement to your parade. They are easy to transport. They can be delivered by UPS to a house or business. They can be used in several ways: walking short parades, entertaining the crowds prior to parades, on floats or in vehicles such as pick-up trucks, convertibles or golf carts.
>
> "The basic cost of rental is low and often local businesses can sponsor the cost. They are easy to operate and can make use of volunteers, which are usually more plentiful than money.
>
> "There are a wide variety of the WalkAround costumes available and something can be found that will fit in with any theme."

Dee Ann Bowen
Omaha, Nebraska
Signs & Shapes International

Power Lines

How many power lines are across your parade route? The spectators won't be aware of the power lines unless they are nearby. They like the excitement when tenders bend the inflatable down to avoid power lines or weave through the traffic signals. They are simply part of the show.

Scout Troops

Boy Scouts, Girl Scouts and other affiliated organizations love to be in a parade. A scout chairperson for this group usually comes from one of the involved parents at a level higher than scout leader. Check with your regional directors. They are looking to recruit more scouts from your spectators in return.

A couple contacted my office multiple times, saying they had to deliver their application to me personally. They were adamant that they would not mail, email or fax their entry. Upon accepting their application, I inquired why it was so important to meet with me. They wanted me to hear this story first-hand. "A child came up to our Scout entry and said 'I don't know who you are or what you do, but I want to be a part of it.'"

That is the impact an entry can have in a parade.

Animal Entries

Equestrian units and their performances can leave the spectators in awe. If you allow live animals, ask your local animal control officer to chair this. They are connected with so many organizations it will make your head spin. Animals improve your parade and you might even find a few "exotics" like camels and elephants. Long-horn cattle are breathtaking to watch in a parade but, like the rest of the animals, they might need to be parade trained. Zoos and animal orphanages can be contacted, but you will need to handle their concerns that the parade could involve cruelty to animals. Insurance is another issue, make sure you're covered.

Remember, if your parade route is a hot surface, use a water truck to cool down the street for the hooves and paws.

Clubs

This can be everything from book clubs, to 4H, car clubs and the Elks. Check your mayor's office and the chamber of commerce for a list of who's who in the community.

Academic School Groups

Refer to them as academic because otherwise you'll get calls from dance schools demanding to be in your free school classification. Dance schools and similar are businesses.

Check in with your regional school administrator. Ask to be put on their agenda for ten minutes at a regularly scheduled meeting with all the local principals in your area and pitch what you want to do.

After the first year in the parade, the schools become competitive between themselves, improving your parade even more. One first grade class carried a sign, "The class of 2024." The spectators roared as they went by.

Don't Call Them Churches

This is politically incorrect. They are houses of worship.

Individuals/Families

You may want this classification for such entries as as an old-time tractor or some other interesting unit with a lot of parade tradition. This applies also to baby stroller or bicycle competitions.

Military Entries

The U.S. military can provide other entries for your parade, including troops, color guard, equipment and other assets. Download the Request for Armed Forces Participation in Public Events (Non Aviation) form.

Other Government Entries

This category is defined as entities with 50 percent or more funding directly or indirectly by tax dollars. Examples are cities, counties, libraries, special taxing districts and open space agencies.

Check your ratio of government entries against the rest. Are 15 percent of the parade entries government entities? They want exposure to your captive audience just like everyone else, and get the same benefits as a business or club.

Political Entries

Giving these entries separate titles will help you with future issues or debates.

So controversial are political entries that some private parades simply don't allow them. Sometimes they even eliminate government or government-related entries, including all of the ones discussed below.

Check to see if this applies to your parade entries: According to 501(c)(3) of the Internal Revenue Code, tax-exempt organizations are prohibited from participating or intervening in political activities.

Political Candidates
Depending on the date of your parade and the next election, having political candidates could also become a controversial issue. Candidates often want to be in the parade and it's been traditional in the past.

Many political groups try to band together in one unit to skirt your fees. Make your applications for each individual candidate. If that has been tradition, send them an email about the new rules or call them many months in advance.

Ballot Issues

These are a tax, bond, laws or some economic issue on an upcoming election. We were outsmarted at a recent parade on a bond issue. They had their entry and that was fine but they put support for their cause on tee shirts that were worn by hundreds of adults and children. They said they had no control of them joining the entry. How do we as parade marshals suggest that children can't march because of the advertising on tee shirts? The election won. No way to figure out who to bill for the political entry.

Political Issues

Spectators' least favorite units are the anti- or pro- groups. As mentioned, citizens are bombarded with issues day in and out, and they come to your parade to get away.

5. PARADE LINE-UP

Simply put, your line-up can make or break the parade. Here are some scripts other parade committees have used when contacting entries.

- The order is determined by the parade Review Committee to establish variety and to ensure the even flow of the parade.
- Please explain the reason for your request. (While efforts will be made to accommodate your requests, there are no guarantees.)
- Only applications by groups or individuals with special circumstances or special needs will be considered.
- Placement. We reserve the sole right to place parade participants in any order deemed appropriate.
- Placement is not on a first-come, first-served basis. Entries will receive their parade order number on the day of the event.

When planning your line-up, keep in mind...

Some marching bands may be traveling long distances to get there and a later starting time might work better. Another solution is to place these bands toward the end of the parade.

Fire trucks blowing their horns and sirens next to a marching band or a unit with music distracts from both entries.

How many entries have music? Which ones have animals? How big is the unit? Having one hundred fifty horses performing can take up several blocks. How many people and how much space does the unit take up?

Layout for a parade with two hundred entries can take one person many hours trying to figure out how they should be spread out. Some parade chairs might be using the date-in stamp to decide. There may be a better way.

Oftentimes the high school students will follow their band, then the middle school or junior high and finally the elementary school. Row after row of students, scout troops or elected officials becomes boring. Let them know your reasons for breaking up the monotony in the line-up early. They may be making promises or discussing this with each other. They will understand.

This goes for other similar groups as well. If you have a bunch of similar-looking units in size, shape, theme or color, space them out to create balance.

One way to start is by stacking or sorting the entry forms into groups. Marching bands, musical entries, schools, scouts, political, houses of worship, entries the spectators might like, animals and the rest. Then rate them.

Putting lots of great entries together means that a lot of poor ones will be grouped together as well. Evenly spacing the different types of entries will work well for the spectators and they won't get bored.

Parents should not walk along the parade route with their children, as children are more likely to behave and follow instructions from adults other than their parents.

Children parades should not exceed two hours so they don't get bored. Nor should the young children have to stay in the staging area too long.

Putting musical units next to each other drowns out both and the spectators cannot appreciate what either unit did.

Also spread out sponsors, if they have multiple vehicle entries, in between other units.

Line up each band about one-hundred-fifty feet away from each other because the students in the front of the band won't be able to hear their band play. The ones in the back only hear the band behind the student, creating lots of footwork errors for everyone. Consider putting paid politicians near marching bands to give them extra value. Add other entries that don't have music to fill the space. If that's not possible, put paid politicians next to a music unit rather than the louder marching band. Same concept applies to your sponsors.

Valerie Lagauskas, formerly with the Macy's Day Parade, makes sense when she says in the IFEA's Official Guide to Parades to lead with a great entry to set the tone and finish the same way, leaving the spectators with a warm feeling for next year.

Shriners say they don't need to be at the end of the parade like a Santa Claus. Spectators stay regardless. So if you want them, mention their better location and watch how many more units show up.

Some parade committees group nonprofit organizations before their commercial entries. Won't this give the spectators a reason to leave early?

Who *Should* Lead?

So many choices, but is it time to change the tradition? Rotate it? Sometimes it's the fire department, a grand marshal or, my favorite, a marching band.

If you have a banner, should that unit lead? Your honor guard might disagree. So let one of them lead and put the other one at least fifty feet back for proper impact? It's a coveted spot.

Is the End the Best Position?

Think of the way people attend parades. When do they show up? Don't they usually just trickle in? A large attendance is gathered at the start and then more come. Even more arrive as friends and family members call others to remind them. Some potential spectators who are in their vehicles see the commotion and stop. Others simply show up late. Many parade participants will also stay to watch the rest of it when they are done performing.

Yes, in my view, the end of the parade is where the best attendance is.

6. PARADE STAGING

When your staging is done well, your parade really shines. Alternatively, a poorly staged parade won't rise above mediocrity.

When Do You Cancel?

Having serious weather conditions makes deciding on cancellation easy, but what about the other weather issues that can arise? As the late Tim Montgomery, our former parade chair, once said, "If there is just one child on the curb, that child will get a parade."

You already know this but to give you more confidence, light rain doesn't stop a parade. If there is heavy rain, hail or lightning close to start time of the parade, delay for thirty minutes and then decide.

It occurs to me that if you do delay, the units will still get wet and the spectators will start leaving if they don't see the parade coming down the street.

Neighborhood Notification

It's becoming politically correct for larger parades to tip off the neighbors that they will be adversely affected both in the staging area and along the parade route, even though your parade may have been going that route for decades.

With notification, it's hard for someone to argue that they didn't know even if they recently moved in. Most parades are often a long-term tradition, like most holidays.

There is some sound reasoning for letting neighbors know, however. As mentioned earlier, people will just plain forget and plan parties or appointments during the times that you have closed the streets or taken up the parking spaces.

Another reason to mention the parade to the neighbors is that some will have special needs or emergencies to prepare for. Some, when reminded, might even spend the night elsewhere to avoid the traffic. All in all, most will welcome your parade with open arms. Who can resist all the positive activity, the music, the excitement? Most neighbors love it, many will even invite friends or family over to watch from their great spot.

Ask your city to give their suggestions on what should be done, as this *can* become political quickly. A few residents and businesses will be NIMBY's, "Not in my backyard." They need to be heard but most communities will have empathy. Make accommodations accordingly or negotiate with community officials to hammer out an arrangement that will work for both. In the end you can't please everyone, and some issues just cannot be minimized.

When sending out notices or reminders about the parade, check with your post office for bulk mail and zip code geographic zones. There's no need to put individual names on the postcard; Dear Resident will do. Often the city or a local Realtor will be able to email you a list.

Use the postage-printed post office postcards for notification and, to be on the safe side, add the location and, if it's very political, time of a meeting at which people can bring up their grievances. You only need to print on one side if you put your return mail address in the message. State the activity, day of the week, hours and date. Add voice mail phone numbers, an address, fax numbers and email address to contact you.

Listen to the responses. Hold a meeting via the postcard if it's very controversial. They need to vent even if there isn't anything else you can do. Others will have a legitimate issue that you may just be able to deal with on parade day.

One of the residents' objections might be medical access. You will actually have more Emergency Medical Service (EMS) people in the area because of the event. Often the EMS will be on a motorcycle, bicycle, golf cart or an ATV. This typically reduces response times during your parade.

Send the postcard notification four to seven days before your parade.

When to Send Staging Letters

If your entries are starting to contact you to find out where and when and what their line-up number is, you now know it's time to have deadlines or move your current one earlier.

This allows you to put information out to the entries in a timely fashion. They in turn need to communicate with the members of their unit. Many will need to know at least ten days in advance and large groups two weeks.

Doing this online saves a lot of time, trouble and expense.

In your staging letter you will need to stress that they cannot change positions. Many will move for their own convenience. Let them know that, according to the rules they will be disqualified if they don't have permission. In addition, the judging cannot take place and the emcees cannot find their scripts when out of order.

Headquarters

Mention where you will set up your headquarters. Having a headquarters during the parade, and keeping someone there throughout the event, is critical. Many VIP'S and media reps will show up and need direction.

Safety in Your Staging Area

Your responsibility is to protect the motorists and participants from potentially hurting some unwitting, happy go lucky parade participant who thinks the entire street is closed and never thinks about traffic and is injured.

You should have three small barricades to stop traffic from entering. One small metal, three-foot barricade isn't enough. Check with your traffic department for permitted types. The Cheyenne Frontier Days parade puts a parade marshal at both ends of an eight-foot wooden barricade. They can tell drivers how best to get to their destination. Have them bring chairs or stools.

Make your own barricades. First take one to show your community traffic department for permission to use. Some will require that you construct it to the uniform code for barricades. However, you may not have to follow the same codes for a daytime barricade.

Some parades might need a hundred or so barricades. They can be knocked down and stored outside under a tarp for next year.

Smaller city halls might allow traffic cones or caution tape across the intersections. Don't forget, you are growing, so even though barricades may not apply to you, they will be needed or appropriate in the future. Add this to your "vision" budget.

Get an Aerial Map

Get or buy one huge, colored aerial map of your staging area and parade route (from your city or Google Earth) and you will see the staging world a little differently. It will give you much better insights on how to improve. All kinds of ideas will pop up once you see the big picture and focus. Ours is a 2 foot x 3 foot color one from the city.

Study the maps for open areas, fields where cars can park, cemeteries with unused land, houses of worship parking lots, private land and commercial parking lots behind the buildings.

Look for your "envelope." An envelope is the area within the newly directed high traffic areas. Keeping your entries and line-up within the envelope eliminates all kinds of problems when having to cross what are now very busy streets.

Try to limit the number of non-unit vehicles allowed to park in the staging area. The parade marshals will be of help here.

Ask your traffic department to post "no parking" signs in your staging area the day before. Most won't tow a vehicle, but many police departments will run the plate and call the owner to see if they can move it on the day of the parade.

Large inflatables will need a larger space to set up and maybe even security.

Many fire departments are now trending toward you using only one side of the street, to allow them to pass.

If you're large enough, put a marshal with each unit. Or assign them to a zone of a block or so. These marshals must have authority. It's hard for young people to stand up to an adult—who decides that he or she doesn't like his position, and moves forward. At best move back those units that request moving so the emcees can find their entry dialogue.

Reducing Gridlock

After the parade starts, some of the units don't move for a while. Stagger the unit check-in times according to their line-up position if it's practical. If you keep them waiting, some will be reluctant to return in future years. Be sure you have not blocked off all access once the parade starts.

On the other hand, if your parade is small, don't worry about having the units there an hour beforehand. Simply note the time the parade starts and let the entries know that it's their responsibility to be on time. This can work well and will take the pressure and responsibility off of you.

Make sure all entries are in place by the time you close the parade route. Some close the parade route fifteen to sixty minutes beforehand. Often the parade chair makes the decision. Sometimes it's in the parade permit.

In your instructions, tell the units which streets to use to get to their location. This will minimize their driving through additional congested streets. Ask them to also stress this as they communicate with their participants. Without good instructions, individuals from the units sometimes show up not knowing their unit number or location. Often they won't know the unit name: "I'm with the scouts," they might say and you have six scout entries at six different locations.

With a fire station in the staging area, ask what access you need to leave open. Check with them yearly as the chiefs or agreements might change. If your parade or staging area encompasses streets around them, suggest they park (stage) some of the trucks outside the perimeter of the parade area for easy response. Tell your community traffic and police department what you want to do. Oftentimes those things that are important to you can be negotiated.

Making two-way streets temporarily one-way can be tough and often unsafe.

Would putting the animals in a location a little farther away and then bringing them up only at parade time work better? Large floats and entries with elderly might also need more staging space. That gives these entries plenty of space to load, access for parking their vehicles and leisurely time to get well organized. Being in a cramped, congested place isn't appropriate for older age groups.

Our band units include sixty school buses and twenty or so equipment buses and some nineteen hundred students. We received permission to use a movie theater parking lot for the staging of the bands and alternate them into the parade route with the rest of the entries from a residential area. We made the theater a sponsor without their knowledge and they loved it. They took pictures and no doubt sent it to their home office.

A lot of parades use sticks or signs to identify their staging locations. If you're using residential streets, consider addresses as GPS tracking and Google Maps are now widely used. You can also put six or seven units per street corner to meet at to align them on that block.

Have a Mandatory Meeting?

Line-up numbers, maps and instructions can be issued at this meeting and questions answered. The purpose for a mandatory meeting is also to eliminate gridlock, confusion and reinforcing the rules. This only applies to larger parades.

Inspection of Entries

Often the rules will spell out that no alcohol or guns are allowed. Sometimes it's to make sure that the unit isn't trying to outsmart the entry fees by adding other advertising into their unit.

An animal control officer can check the health of animals in staging, and not necessarily cite the owners but suggest to them that the animal needs to see a vet. Many communities require that some animals be licensed. Ask your jurisdiction if this would be enforced here.

Fire departments can check for float safety.
Make sure the entries understand they must keep their staging area cleaned up.

What Time Do You Close the Parade Route?

This depends on the size of your parade and if you have any planned pre-parade entertainment.

Most medium-sized parades close streets fifteen to thirty minutes beforehand to give the police time to clear traffic.

Many municipalities will close the entire parade route, no matter how long your route is, all at the same time for spectators' safety. The spectators are showing up in the gutters and they want to give everyone better protection along a busy street. Others will close the streets in stages.

General Safety

You have a responsibility to the spectators. Please review the June 2011 Protective Measures Guide for the U.S. Outdoor Venues Industry and any follow-up information they offer. It's from Homeland Security. Many communities now have a staff person who covers catastrophes and emergency preparedness that each year you should check in with.

Command Center

At the time of the parade, the assistant chair, police and fire departments should be the command center at an elevated place to be able to view most of the parade route. Allow the parade marshals on every block to be in constant contact. As you grow, consider having a zone manager for several blocks that the parade marshals report to and these zone managers should stay in touch with the command center. This way, when anything happens, the communications are fast and those further down the parade route will be in the loop before a problem reaches them. Do not locate them at your headquarters.

Are you politically ready for a serious problem? It's coming. You just don't know when, where or what. Do you have press releases done for such things? Do you know not to stop or cancel the parade if someone dies or is severely injured, as it's confined to that area? Keep a staff member with the individual to the hospital. Send another to that individual's home to inform or pick up family members. Stay on top of the problem and constantly keep the media informed or someone or worse the media will take control away from you. Afterwords, follow up and stay in touch for what else you can do.

Log Jam?

For your parade to be a success, the disband area also needs to be a smooth operation. Many parades experience a jam at the end of the parade because the entries stop to unload, or they have no place to go and just hang out there. Your planning, parade marshals and rules can assist and fix this.

Decide which way each type of unit goes at the end. Maybe floats and vehicles go one direction and marchers go a different one.

7. JUDGING PARADE ENTRIES

Life is a parade of ongoing accolades that should be acknowledged throughout one's journey.

Judy Flanagan CFEE, MS
Professional speaker and consultant
She has directed special events and parades for Walt Disney World and has been involved with Macy's Thanksgiving Day Parade

A discussion on improving parades would not be complete without covering the issues of judges, awards and bragging rights.

Eliminate Judging?

Entries get emotional over judging. Most want to win but only a few can. Some of the losers will be annoyed. Coming in second can even cause hurt feelings. So consider whether judging is right for your parade.

One camp thinks all entries get enough value and attention from just being in the parade and that no judging needs to take place.

Some parades can't afford the judges or the prize money and plaques.

Sometimes it depends on the income from the entries. If most of your entries are free and you're giving out a trophy, that's great. For many parades this is their largest expense and they can't afford it.

With an "Animal Parade" theme, how do you compare the enjoyment of seeing twenty horses and riders doing their great routines to the impact of viewing at eye level dozens of long-horn cattle while seated on a curb?

Some groups simply don't want to be judged, so call them an Exhibition Unit. This gives them due respect and the spectators won't wonder why they are not being judged.

We asked our city's Cultural Arts Center to do the judging for us. It added more dignity to the parade. We allowed for first and second places. We were surprised that several entries could have won in several categories. To avoid changing the results, we created a Chairman's Award, which is above the first place for those six entries that received very high scores on more than one classification.

Every other entry that wished to be judged was awarded a nice Honorable Mention ribbon ($6). You must take care of your entries for them to return next year.

Judging Criteria

If there is judging, should it be via a published or non-published list of criteria of how the entries are going to be judged? Would publishing create fewer issues? The Arlington 4th of July Association and the Pacific Coast Judges Association have some interesting ideas on criteria.

- Artistry
- Beauty
- Best Presentation of Spirit
- Best Craftsmanship
- Best Overall
- Creativity
- Effectiveness
- Entertainment Value
- Innovation
- Interpretation of the Theme
- Judges Award
- Most Original
- Overall Quality
- Special Effects
- Use of Theme
- Visual Effect

More Thoughts on Judging

Here are some comments from other parade committees:

- Judges' criteria is/is not available to participants.
-
- Judges' criteria depends on whether the judges want the units to see them ahead of time or not.

- Judging location as to where and when it will take place needs to be communicated.

- Equestrian and float judging is/is not done on the parade route.

To improve your parade you need credible judges. Maybe not use the locals who have done it for years.

How do you define qualified judges and the criteria? Look at the types of entries. Then think about which groups might be appropriate to judge them.

Another way to find float judges and criteria is to ask those in charge of making theater sets. They will likely be thrilled to do it. Art teachers are also a good resource. We tried this with great results. They served as judges and auditors, who tallied the results.

These outreaches add credibility to your parade. Posting the criteria and noting how qualified the judges are will improve your parade and gain more respect. For privacy sake, you might not want to give their actual names.

Another way to find these is to ask the entries in each classification who you should pick on a professional level.

For dancing, go to your performing art centers and ask them to do the judging. Dance studios, ballroom, tap, and freestyle all have their own set of biases. Bring the dance judges together to decide which criteria are appropriate.

Your parks and recreation staff might be able to give suggestions as to which teachers to contact.

Ask the qualified judges to set the criteria based on their expertise. Host a meeting with the judges and last year's entries and have them work it out together. Submit details on what other parades are doing criteria-wise and let them edit it.

Marching band directors, in particular, don't want to be judged by someone who lacks serious knowledge. Bands and marching bands in general are easier to judge because their industry has many different standards you can use. Ask the band directors to meet and hammer out how it should be done together. High school band associations in your state can help with this issue as well.

Consider that you may need six band judges, two each for music, marching and overall effect.

You might also work toward announcing the rest of the award winners at the same time. Needless to say, we were delinquent one year, in getting them out and learned that sooner is better and shortly thereafter is best, even if no one shows up.

Some professional people may want to be paid to judge, especially marching band judges. Band judges can run from $50 to $250 each for credible, high caliber and prestigious judges. Factor this in when setting up your entry fees.

Some judging of units and performing units are judged or prejudged in the staging area, prior to the start of the parade, sometimes by non-identified judges.

Many parades post a sign or paint a line on the street showing the start and end of the judging area.

As you put all of this into place, think of how much you just improved the parade. How many more entries will come because of the better judging? Think about how much more work they will now put into their unit because of this.

Awards

Awards are expensive and need to be factored into the entry fees as well. The types of awards are staggering from certificates, money, trophies and ribbons.

Consider not having the ceremony right after the parade since everyone will have dispersed. If you're using plaques they may need to be inscribed after a ceremony. Having a ceremony later is a lot cheaper than trying to mail or hand-deliver the awards later. Or simply have them picked up at your office.

Present the awards at a City Council or community meeting to further enhance your parade. Often it can be filmed on your community cable channel.

You may need to give something out to gain stature and thank the entries for coming. Buy 25-cent participant ribbons and deliver them in your staging areas.

Please check **Appendix I**, for what may need to be communicated for your awards.

MISCELLANEOUS

It was a "real" parade!

OK, the parade is over and you can let out a big sigh of relief. Now to assess the quality of this year's parade before you move on to other activities. Do you need bragging rights? You know what you have done and there is no way that it can be known other than by other parade chairs and their committees. Instead of tooting your own horn, let others define what you have done. Not broadcasting it makes you shine with the more sophisticated people in your community, who may not know all of what you have done but they know from their own life experiences it was a lot more than they could have imagined. When they say it was a "real parade," you know you're well on your way.

I have talked a lot about how important it is to plan ahead because parades are rarely a one-time event and you will want to capitalize on what you've learned. Here are some additional thoughts.

Next Year

Start your meetings a year beforehand and brainstorm last year's parade. Then meet frequently over the next two months setting up the changes and implementing all of your new ideas for next year. Start your quest for entries.

Pay close attention to any complaints about the parade. You can assume any comments are being echoed by many others outside of your earshot. It won't take long to think of a way to fix or improve on it no matter how insignificant.

Create new budgets based on your unexpected expenses or incomes.

Don't wait to meet and implement new ideas and changes. Everyone is excited and energized right after a parade. A few months or even weeks later they will have moved on to something else. So act quickly. Then take six months off, checking voice and email every week or so. Four months beforehand start the meetings once again as you get closer to parade day. It will be obvious to you how frequent the meetings need to be.

Often the city will send in a crew afterward to blow the trash from the sidewalk to the streets. Then street sweepers pick it up. Be sure the route is cleaned up as the businesses and homeowners will remember you next year in a positive light.

As you improve your parade, adjust your vision with all the new thoughts and ideas generated. Parades are dynamic and evolving. When you look back, you may not recognize your earlier parades.

Handling Growth

As your parade grows and gets more attention, it's only natural that many will want to be a part of it. Some will want to control it, others will want their visions to be your visions. They may be forceful about this, having recognized how powerful a parade can be.

Now is the time to reflect. If you have political problems now, it may be because you didn't have a two-year chair policy in place and that chair didn't move on to another chair position. Often they have taken ownership of the position.

The grander your parade becomes, the bigger the target you are.

One way to handle any political moves is by listening, defending your position and then letting go. Let them air their points of view and evaluate whether their ideas improve your parade or the big picture. Be generous with your praise.

No matter what, there will always be people who don't want you to succeed. This is true with everything in life. With parades, this can be because you, in effect, are taking away a bit of their standing in the community as a leader. You are the one receiving the praise.

Some will want to take over your position or perhaps gain undeserved credit. Others might want to push their ideas on you, suggesting that their plans for "bigger and better" should be listened to and augmented. Everyone has big ideas, but you are in the position to know if any of those grandiose ideas will actually improve your parade.

Stick to your new vision.

Or, if you need help, for a $25 hourly fee, I'd be happy to be your consultant. Additionally, if you need ideas on youth parades, please contact me. I believe youth parades are the future.

Final Thoughts...

This guidebook may not have the rush of winning a close ball game, and it doesn't pretend to be able to answer every question. It's simply my way to share ideas and tips to improve your parade. Thank you for your patience with my efforts to bring to print that which most of us are doing from memory, experience and shooting from the hip. I hope this has added to your confidence that you're already doing it well.

Ed C. Tomlinson

APPENDICES

A Parade Chair Titles
B Rarely Asked Parade Permit Application Questions & Observations
C Professional Looking Forms
D Improving Your Application
E Release of Liabilities
F Signatures
G Types of Entry Classifications
H Classification of Non-Band Rules
I Awards

Appendix A Parade Chair Titles

ADA Americans with Disabilities
Animal Entries
Audio Equipment
Bands
Bleachers
Celebrities
Commercial Entries
Communications
Concessions
Cultural Entries
Dancers
Dignitaries
Eco-Friendly
Elected Officials
Emcees
Fire Department
Float Support
Fund Raising
Future Shuttles
Gofer
Grandstand
Judging
Media
Military Entries
New Entries
Olympics
Pancake Breakfast.
Parking
Police Liaison
Pre-Parade Entertainment
Public Relations
Reviewing Stands
School Entries
Scout Entries
Senior Citizens
Social Networks
Sponsors
Staging
Tall Inflatables
Television
Traffic
Volunteers
Website

Appendix B Rarely Asked Parade Permit Application Questions and Observations

Application Questions

- Will the parade cross any railroad tracks?
- Will the parade be using the entire right of way?
- Space in between participant entries or vehicles.
- Is this parade political in nature?
- Has the applicant ever been convicted of any crime?
- Has the applicant been denied any permit in the past?

Application Observations

The time required for application before the parade is typically between two days and four weeks. At least one city requires six months. A New York legal ruling thought that 30 days was too long.

City response times to your applications are two days to three months.

A copy of your contract for barricades is usually needed. Some communities charge $3 each. In many communities the barricades are free, but you must supply the volunteers to pick them up from city shops and deliver them to the streets for the traffic department deployment. It's best to let the city people do it as sometimes it will be incomplete and the community traffic and police departments may get angry.

About 40 percent of the applications want to know how many animals, and floats.

"Is this to be held by, or on behalf of or for any person other than applicant" is asked 70 percent of the time.

Loud-sound systems are often frowned upon.

The permit is for public rights of way only; this includes streets, alleys and sidewalks, not private property.

Guidelines and rules can be negotiated.

Insurance typically is $1 million; some want three.

About half offer an appeal process without going to court.

Most will let you know if a stipend for police is appropriate.

About 20 percent want an indemnification and hold-harmless agreement.

Nonrefundable permit fees typically run $10-$25. Some charge $50 and a couple at $100.

Supply volunteers to monitor barricades.

No parking zone sign, fees.

Some communities have ordinances forbidding any outsiders from interfering in the parade.

Fire departments float inspections.

Appendix C Professional Looking Forms

An evaluation of nearly one thousand parade websites underscores the need in the parade industry for review of the seventy-five different forms being used. Someone might have a better list than I, but the following titles might be a start to help us communicate better with our entries through easy-to-understand terms and consistency. The ten suggested titles are Application, Entry Fees, Rules, Release of Liability, Authorizations, General Information, Staging Instructions, Judging Criteria, Classifications and Awards.

Tell the reader which time zones are being used.

Putting the date on each form will allow you to determine which edition is the most current. As you change the forms, midstream, the old ones, if utilized by a unit, are grandfathered in.

Put contact information on each page. Many pages are out of order, tossed or passed around.

Keep a copy of this page for your records.

Many parade forms are crowded, with little white space. Having an inviting form creates a more valuable relationship with your various entities. Here is a chance to get creative; use photos or clip art to dress them up and make them more interesting.

Always remember to add the date along with a signature.

Put your larger sponsors' names on each page.

Appendix D Improving Your Application

When you say "no" to applicants that don't fit in, don't be surprised when they come back after they make improvements to the quality of their unit.

Your Mission Statement

Use these to start or end your page. Here are some examples of using a mission statement for a more polished image:

"The Miracles Christmas Parade exists to bring cheer to every spectator, participant and organizer and to provide families and individuals an event that will build lasting holiday memories. The Miracles Parade is produced by a group of community volunteers that donate their time."

Terms

Add parade start times, theme, day of the week and date of the parade.

Add your parade dates for the next three years. Many military units, sponsors, national and corporate entries need to know this for effective planning, helping you get better entries.

Application deadlines often appear at the top of the page in the header. Some parade committees have mellowed the word "deadline" with:

- Applications can be submitted until...
- Applications are taken/accepted until...
- Sorry, absolutely no exceptions after...

Invitation Paragraphs

Personalize and create atmosphere and mood like these:

The parade committee is honored you are applying to be in our parade. We are working hard to make this a smooth and easy day for you. You are important to us.

Welcome parade applicants!

The Parade Committee cordially invites your organization...

"...encourages your application for the Dr. Martin Luther King Jr. parade. The Tampa, Florida parade has continued to grow and improve in quality and content since its inception. Participating in this event is not only great fun but it also provides you with an excellent way to promote your organization at minimal cost. Entries are limited, so please submit your application early."

"The National Cherry Blossom Festival® is seeking marching bands to participate in the parade. The parade is a complex mix of entertainment including gigantic balloons, magnificent floats, specialty units, celebrity talent, and production numbers. Marching bands are an integral part of the mix; the pageantry, music selections, colors, marching style, and auxiliary contributions help create a stunning presentation."

"The crisp, fall air and the turning of leaves bring a Coulee Region tradition...the Oktoberfest Maple Leaf Parade! Even after forty years, thousands of families and friends get together lining the two-mile route in La Crosse with their lawn chairs, snacks and refreshments and enjoy a 2+ hour parade winding through the city."

"Oktoberfest illuminated event, the Torchlight Parade, brings sparkle and light to La Crosse's Northside. Fantastic floats, marching bands and unique specialty units combine to transform the quiet Northside neighborhood into a magical showpiece of color and excitement."

"On behalf of the Alpenfest Grand Parade Committee, I would like to invite you to participate in the next Alpenfest Grand Parade. We need you to make this year's parade better than ever."

Welcome, Parade Applicants! We realize this is a lot to read and digest, but it is for your own safety as participants, as well as the safety of the spectators.

On behalf of the xxx Parade Committee, I would like to invite you to...

We invite your organization to participate in this year's parade.

We sincerely appreciate your interest in our community and hope your organization will participate in this year's parade.

An Application Is Information to Make Your Decision on

Many parades limit the number of entries. Often the number quoted is from eighty to two hundred. This allows an orderly parade. Limiting the number of any specific type of entry is common to encourage, discourage or create balance. This keeps you in control and creates urgency.

The following are phrases that you might consider using for your application.

Examples of Application Wording

Applications will be evaluated between xx-xx

You will receive notification of acceptance or rejection by mail or email.

When approved you will be notified by xx, by way of...

Upon approval you will be emailed a line-up time...

A confirmation will be emailed to you.

No reminders will be mailed.

The Parade Director will confirm your parade registration by telephone or email. If you've not received a confirmation by...we do not have a completed application. If this occurs, please contact...immediately.

Entry to the parade is by invitation only.

Those interested in participating must send photos, videos or audio clips, along with the application. Electronic submission is preferred. All applications are organized by the AFIC and presented to the Presidential Inaugural Committee, whose members ultimately select the participants. The Presidential Inaugural Committee can also re-extend the application submission form.

The following is all the information you need to apply for participation in either Oktoberfest Parade. Even if you've participated in the parades in the past, please read all information carefully. Requirements do change from year to year and it is the responsibility of each unit to comply. Past participation in either parade does not guarantee acceptance for the next parade.

Contact person.

Number of children under 18?

Submit detailed drawing of how your unit is expected to look.

Please do/do not send payment with your application.

There are two methods of entering this year's grand parade...

The person authorized to act in behalf of applicant if other than above...

The person who will be onsite and in charge of conducting the parade unit and will be responsible to city official employees for ensuring that the parade is conducted in compliance with this year's parade rules and other applicable laws.

Additional contact.

Work phone.

Best time to reach you.

Day of parade, phone.

How long has your organization been in existence?

Please describe the reason your organization would like to appear in the parade.

Please supply any other information that will help the parade producers to evaluate your application.

Is this your first time in the parade?

How many years have you been in the parade?

Is your group a military organization?

Name of your organization's president/chair/CEO.

Where are your organization's main offices?

Previous parade awards received.

No faxed applications accepted.

Photos must accompany all commercial units.

Each unit must submit an individual application fee.

Photographs are encouraged.

Materials used on the float...

What will your costumes look like?

Is your float animated?

Entries must be of entertainment value.

Do not include information about this unit to the website or the media. (Check box)

Is this a royalty-riding float?

Applications to be in the parade will not be considered if fees from last year remain unpaid.

Any non-commercial parade entity is responsible to specifically name the driver of the vehicle and provide a description of their vehicle, then submit a copy of their personal auto insurance card with their parade entry application.

The parade committee expressly reserves the right to reject the application of any organization whose float, message or participants, at the sole discretion of the parade committee, is considered potentially disruptive, offensive or in poor taste and not in keeping with the tradition of the Marigold Festival parade.

Open to all, but the committee reserves the right to limit and screen entries based on a group's service to the community.

Riverton City reserves the right to deny an application if we determine an entry to be controversial, unlawful or otherwise considered to be inconsistent with the standards or the purpose of the Riverton City Town Days Parade.

Your application does not suggest acceptance.

The number of parade entries will be limited to X units. First consideration will be given to entries that best match the parade theme. Second consideration will be given to returning entries.

The parade committee will, subject to space, legal, and safety considerations, endeavor to accommodate all parade applications that are eligible under the categories contained in this entry kit. Apply early! We expect all available categories contained in this entry kit be allocated by 2010.

"Again this year we are limiting the number of parade entries to xxx units. This will allow for a shorter, higher quality, and better-managed parade. Unfortunately, it also means we will not be able to accommodate everyone wishing to participate in the parade." Oktoberfest Maple Leaf Parade

Band Applications

Include:

Description of band uniforms.

Unit awards/recognition's, notable history or performances.

Please submit a DVD of your band performance in at least one parade appearance.

A color photograph of the organization.

Color photographs of your uniforms.

Your band's biography.

Marching bands must have a membership of X to be considered.

Please list three references who can endorse the performance quality of your band

Music Applications

Will your unit have music?

Low noise generators, rated for musical sound systems must be used.

Sound selection.

Style.

Boom box.

Live music.

Vocals.

Announcements.

Musical selection.

Music title.

Will you be using a sound system for your unit? yes__ no__?
Live Music__ Taped Music__ Loud Speaker__ No Music__

If yes, how will your sound system be moved along the parade route?

Send one recording via DVD, CD or an emailed MPEG.
Mark all recordings with the name of the group, the director, the city and the date of the recording.

Closed Applications

No entries accepted after...

Late entries will be accepted as resources and time permit.

Applications for the 2009 parade are CLOSED.

Thank You...

Thank you for applying to the...

The parade looks forward to receiving your application!

We look forward to your participation in another great ______ parade.

If you're aware of other area civic or veterans' organizations that might be interested in participating in the parade, we would appreciate a call so information can be sent to them.

Appendix E Release of Liabilities

The following are examples of liability issues and terminology.

Some of these documents are called:

General Release(s)
Hold Harmless Agreement
Liability Release Form
Parade Disclosure Affidavit
Parental Consent
Parade Authorization
Participant Disclaimer
Participants Release Form
Release and Indemnification Agreement
Release Form
Release of Liability
Waiver Agreement
Waiver and Release of Damages
Waiver of Participation

(Someone smarter than I, please help our industry to standardize these.—Ed)

Examples of Your Disclaimer

Any political statements or endorsements made by participants in the parade are not necessarily the opinions expressed by us nor do we in any way directly contribute financially to the signage or display of these opinions.

Reserves the right to dismiss...

...Absolved of any activities in association with...

"The Atlanta Pride Committee Inc. hereby absolves any liability arising from use of floats in the Atlanta Pride Committee parade or any activities in association with APC in accordance to City, State, and Federal Laws; no alcoholic beverages will be allowed during any portion of the Pride parade event on November 1, 2009. In addition, no person under the influence of alcohol or drugs shall be allowed to operate a motor vehicle during the Pride parade. APC reserves the right to remove, including but not limited to, any person, motorized or un-motorized vehicle, conveyance, float or participant(s) for any activity deemed unsafe, violation of any rules contained herein, or action or inaction that may cause any delay to the progress of the parade. APC attempts to accommodate all requests for parade placement, however parade placement of participants is at the sole discretion of APC and such placements are final."

"Miracles Christmas Parade is an entertainment event, designed to appeal to families and to bring the community and region together. The parade will not be a forum for intolerance or political messages. As a component of the parade, some of the parade units may be designed to honor the religious significance of the holiday season and the cultural heritage and ethnic diversity of the region. The parade producer, Miracles Christmas Parade, will make decisions at its sole discretion as to the content, design and participants in the parade."

Appendix F Signatures

An actual replica of a chairperson signature is professional looking.

Use electronic buttons on your website: *I do not agree to all terms – I accept all terms* is a good way of proving in court or otherwise, if they have agreed to what is written on the form.

Here is additional wording:

> By signing below, I certify that I have read and understand the application instructions, rules for participating and the parade entry contract. As the primary contact person, I understand I will be the only person to contact to inform the group of important information, dates, and requests for additional information. I further understand that participation in the parade is a privilege and will adhere to the letter, the spirit and the principles of this event. This is a binding contract and I am 18 years of age or older and have been authorized by my sponsoring organization to enter into this contract.
>
> Your application is not complete unless it is signed. Please read and understand all terms and conditions. You're signing a legal binding document."
>
> Signing the application also affirms the applicant is not sponsored by any third-party organization or business. Any waiver of the aforementioned is at the sole discretion of the parade committee and can only be affected by the express written consent of the committee. Please read and sign the appropriate forms.

Appendix G Types of Entry Classifications

Marching Bands

Alumni Corps
College Band
Dance
Drum Corps Style
Drum Corps
Fife/drum Corps
High School Bands
Junior Drum Corps
Military
Senior
Specialty Band
String Band
Traditional Scottish

Band Unit Breakdowns

Flags
Brass
Rifles
Woodwinds
Drum Line

Non-Band Entries

AAAA, AAA, AA, A, B School Sizes
Actors/Singers
Adult
All Star Tap Team
Antique Auto
Antique Entries
Baton
Best Appearing Emergency Unit
Best Appearing Fire Company
Best Appearing School unit
Best Cheerleading Unit
Best Churches and Church Organization
Best Civic /Community
Best Commercial Float
Best Community Float
Best Dance Squad
Best Dance, Marching

Best Entertainment Group (Adult)
Best Entertainment Group (Children)
Best Equestrian 1 or 2 Riders
Best Equestrian 3 or more Riders
Best Equestrian Unit
Best Float, pre kindergarten or early childhood
Best Law Enforcement Unit
Best Military Unit
Best commercial Float
Best non-commercial Float
Best Service Club
Best Sorority and Fraternity
Best Themed Float
Best use of Lights
Best use of Theme
Best Vehicle Group
Business
Car(s)
Chairman's Award or Pick
Clowns
Color Guard
Comedy
Communities under 5,000, 5,000 to 25,000, over 25,000, outside USA
Community Interest
Decorated Car or Truck
Drill Team
Family
Flag Team,
Float with out Music
Float with Live Music
Float with Recorded Music
Homemade
Honorable Mention
Motorcycle
Non profit
Novelty
Political
Politician in Car
Politician Walking
Pooper-Scooper
President's Award
Private
Professional
Royalty

School/Church/Club
Segways
Senior
Social Organization
Special Guests
Specialty Units
Sports Teams
Senior High School
Truck with Trailer
Truck/Van
VFW
VIPs
Visiting Royalty
Walking
Wheeled Unit
Youth Choir

Appendix H Classification of Non-Band Rules

All Entries Rules

This parade is designed for family entertainment.

This is a family and children oriented event.
Do nothing that would compromise this event (profanity, conduct).

The police may confiscate the super soakers.

Once an applicant is selected to participate in the parade; additional units affiliated and/or non-affiliated cannot be added.

A maximum of ten entries in each classification total in parade.

All fees are waived for (those you want to encourage).

Entries are responsible and need to be insured.

No entries advocating, opposing, or depicting political, social, personal or religious issues and agendas; age, creeds, cultures, orientations, sexes, or races; or demean any segment of our society, sexually explicit or suggestive, offensive, national origin, disability or personal characteristics.

Comply with the (you pick the year that your community has enacted) Uniform Fire Code (UFC) Section 1104.

Inherently flame resistant.

Sound amplifying systems should not be played so loudly as to interfere with other units.

The parade cannot be used to further any cause no matter how worthy, whether it is social, religious, political, or commercial.

No water balloons, excessive noise, bells, sirens, fireworks, horns, noise makers, streamers, glitter, pepper sprays, glass bottles, water rifles, super soakers, squirt guns, water guns, silly string, water pistols, poppers, or confetti allowed.

No firing of anything.

No smoking.

There are no refunds, rain dates, doubling up, disorderliness, bad taste or handouts.

Not responsible for theft.

Don't do anything to embarrass the committee.

No entries that do not contribute to the color, visual experience and expression of the parade.

Parade entries limited to xx number of participants.

A parade representative must attend a mandatory pre-parade meeting.

No movement other than forward.

No Santa Clauses.

Maximum widths, lengths and heights of entries.

Decorated in good taste.

A copy of these rules must be in possession by one of your unit participants at all times.

Two years of no shows will be suspended from future parades.

Entrants who violate the rules may be declined in future parades.

Each unit is limited to a 40' X 20' foot print space.

If the unit is different or differs greatly from their application, the unit will not be invited back. (Note—this might be a great rule for some but other groups only need you one year. A few of you might remember what the Beatles said after they did the Ed Sullivan show. When they broke the rules and the producer said they would not be invited back, they responded, "We have already done the Ed Sullivan Show.")

No jumping off and back onto a moving unit.

The designated person in charge will be held responsible for the compliance of the unit as a whole.

No hindrance to the safety or progress of the parade.

All entries must be ready to move on cue at the parade start or the next contingent will proceed. The delayed contingent will proceed only at the next convenient time as determined by the parade marshal.

We reserve the right to revise the placement of all entries.

Deemed to be unsafe.

Units must maintain a forward cadence.

Any parade unit not decorated and participating will not be invited to next year's parade.

Alcohol is prohibited in pre-parade assembly area or the parade route.

The pick-up location for children and other participants must be in a safe location away from the end of the parade.

You must complete the entire parade route.

Glass bottles, balloons filled with anything other than helium or air, body armor, bricks stones, projectile launching equipment including water gun, or operational gas masks.

Do not interfere with other entries.

Entries are asked to stay between 20' and 30' away from each other.

Your unit must depict the parade theme in some manner.

Units for advertisement purposes only will not be accepted.

No pyrotechnics, dangerous acts or sudden noises.

Non-compliance of the rules and regulations could result in future application denials for your organization.

Entries are expected to perform courteously, in good taste and with safety in mind at all times. This includes during the assembly, staging, execution and dispersal of the parade

Sponsors should avoid over-commercialization.

Any commercial message should be a minor part of the float presentation.

Entry Rules Must...

Be reviewed via CD for live TV performances.

Have 1,000 lights for night parades.

Have music, humor, entertainment, costumes or be a sponsor.

Be respectful.

Have water for your group for heat exhaustion and stroke.

Be self-propelled.

Not be self-propelled.

Be designed for viewing from all sides.

Be decorated.

Unit number must be displayed on 8-½ x 11 piece of paper or cardboard in black numbers displayed on windshield, and both sides.

Materials used in each unit should be fire-retardant and not of a dangerous nature.

Vehicle Rules

No more than two or three motorized vehicles per unit.

All vehicles must pre-date year (date)

All vehicles must be built within the last five years.

Good driver vision and ventilation.

Motor vehicles properly licensed and registered, properly serviced with water, gasoline, oil, good working brakes, have tires checked, battery charged.

Towing vehicles must be decorated

Driver, with a key, must be within 20' of steering wheel at all times.

Only a limited number of motorized vehicles will be permitted.

Team buses will not be accepted.

Semi tractors will not be accepted as individual entries.

Licenses and insurance will be verified on the day of the parade.

Pre-parade fire inspection will be at (time of day). Entrants who do not pass all inspections may be removed from the parade.

Excessively large or long trucks (including semi-tractor trailer units) are/are not allowed.

No bare trucks, wagon or trailers will be permitted.

Prior approval is required for go-cart-type vehicles, miniature race cars, or school buses in the parade.

All vehicles shall be clean and polished.

All motorized units must proceed at a slow pace. No speeding up, skidding or sudden breaking will be allowed.

No closed vehicles, i.e., vans and limousines, will be allowed.

Driver must have a 180-degree vision.

Driver must have two spotters, one on each side of float for diminished vision.

Plain vehicles with only a company logo are not permitted.

No ropes, wires and chains shall serve as the primary connection between vehicles.

No one is allowed on a running board, hood, roof or fender.

Driver is solely responsible for damages.

Driver must have a legal driver's license.

Driver must be an adult complying with any state requirements for that type of vehicle with proof of insurance.

All vehicles must be able to navigate the entire parade route, make all turns required without difficulty, and must be able to travel at a speed of at least two miles per hour for the entire parade route.

No vans, motorcycles, scooters, tractor trailers, tractors, mopeds, campers, ATV's, motorized vehicles, wheel chairs, generators, loud motorized vehicles, revving of engines, burning of rubber, wheelies, pocket bikes, or mini-motorcycles.

No motor vehicles.

During the Parade Rules

No mingling or accosting the spectators.

Nothing should be done involving your unit that would encourage spectators to approach the unit.

Entries may not solicit spectators to join your unit.

No activity to entice spectators to enter the parade.

Performances may be done when natural stops occur along the parade route.

No one can get on the unit once it has started down the parade route.

Performances are not allowed to stop the parade.

Drivers must stay within twenty to fifty feet of the unit in front of you.

Performance can only last 10-150 seconds.

Backing up is strongly discouraged.

Stunts and comedy acts must be submitted on a CD prior to acceptance.

Follow instructions of the parade marshals.

Do not stop to unload until you're back in the staging area.

All units must proceed past the end of the parade route before stopping and unloading.

Do not walk back through the parade route after disbanding.

First aid kits are accessible in the line-up area as well as at its dispersal. Paramedics will be on hand if any of your members require first aid.

Marchers Rules

Each ROTC unit should be preceded by its own color guard.

Signage Rules

No printed advertising, logos, advertising of drugs, alcohol or tobacco products.

Only display name of sponsor and parade theme.

Banner carriers must be capable of maintaining the parade pace otherwise the banner may be removed by a parade marshal.

Maximum sign size is 24" X 36."

Signs are not to exceed 18" X 60."

You may use a maximum of three signs.

Use the words "Presented by..."

Flags shall be compliant to standards by U.S. Congress

U.S. Flags are not dipped to any person or thing.

Magnetic signs are encouraged.

Written words or logos must be submitted for approval in a parade participant application to the...

Lettering on the float must not be over six inches in height unless a company logo is incorporated.

Signs and banners must be able to be read from at least 10-50 feet.

Only business entries may display a company name; all others entries must cover the advertising.

The name and/or logo of the sponsor may be displayed on the parade unit but should not detract from the unit.

Band Rules

If the number of playing members changes before the parade date, please notify the parade committee.

Music Rules

Will not interfere with other entries.

All music in the parade must be pre-approved by parade producers.

Please list your musical selection below and enclose a CD with this application.

Please submit a CD by (date) to be considered.

Noise level must not exceed 90 decibels. This includes sirens, air horns and loud engines.

Keep your music turned off in the parking lot prior to start of the parade.

It is ok to check your equipment, but then turn it off so that the volunteers can communicate with you and other entries.

Limited to a five-minute sound check.

Volume must be adjustable.

Sound may not be audible more than thirty feet.

Political Issue Rules

As a 501(c)(3) non-profit status. Due to this non-profit status, we are now required to enforce our parade guidelines that state: The parade is not a platform for addressing public or private issues. Issue-oriented entries will not be accepted. We are required to deny groups that have an objective or goal to influence legislative outcomes.

This is not a platform for political campaigns, social or religious issues or to target special interest groups.

Due to non-compliance of parade rules in past years, absolutely NO handouts of any kind will be allowed along the parade route.

Elected officials or candidates for elected office must personally appear in the unit bearing his/her name. No literature will be allowed to be handed out.

Mayor and city council may enter as one unit.

The Illinois governor, U.S. senators from Illinois or the US Congressman for District 19 may each enter as a separate unit.

All other elected officials and candidates must ride on the float/unit for their party. This includes state senators, state representatives, judges, regional / county offices, and other local offices.

Material deemed controversial by the parade chair and or the parade committee will not be allowed in the parade.

If the unit, in the judgment of the parade chair or members of the committee, is controversial, unlawful, political or otherwise inconsistent with the standards, theme quality or purpose of the parade, it will be removed.

All dignitaries are expected to supply their own vehicles and signage.

During election years, candidates for public office must group with others of their party to design a well-decorated unit promoting the parade theme.

No political campaign literature can be distributed.

No controversial entries.

Dignitaries and politicians must ride.

Dignitaries and politicians must walk.

Fees are per individual.

No doubling up of entries into one unit.

Distribution Rules

If you will be distributing any of the following, submit to the committee for approval all that apply: candy, toys, giveaways, literature, or coupons.

Submit and briefly describe the items(s) that your organization would like to distribute during the parade. Items are limited to...

No tossing.

Must be tossed on the grass beyond the spectators to avoid accidents.

No give-away item may be dropped or thrown from the parade unit.

Please describe if you plan on distributing written information, send sample for approval.

No allowed handouts in front of or behind your unit.

No business flyers can be handed out for advertising purposes.

Only parade sponsors are permitted to pass out anything.

Only walkers can pass out things.

Must be age 14 and older to pass anything out.

No gummy candy or other types of non-wrapped edibles.

Hand-deliver the candy to the spectators.

Walk along the gutter and spread it underhanded within 18" of the curb or behind the spectators.

Handouts must not slow down the parade.

A business may sponsor a balloon man to walk both sides of the street.

Inflatables Rules

Helium parade balloons must not exceed 30 feet long/high by 15 feet wide.

Balloons will not be operated in sustained winds in excess of 23 mpg or gusts of more than 34 mph.

Balloon handlers must be 18 years of age or older and physically capable.

Turn off the blower to deflate the balloon when nearing an overhead problem.

Vendors

Must pre-register.

No sales may occur along the parade route without express written approval of the parade committee. We will patrol the route and identify and remove parade crashers who have not properly registered and are operating illegally.

Staging Rules

Any individual not associated with a parade unit will not be permitted in the staging area.

Staging may give a special consideration for the entries with elderly, children or those with special health needs.

All units must be in their designated line-up position by xxx.

Each unit and vehicle must have an appropriate pass to enter the staging area.

Do not park in line-up area before xxx a.m.

At this time the parade's judges will be walking through the line-up area for a preview of all the units.

We reserve the right to revise the placement of all entries.

Float Rules

Bike riders, inline skates, scooters, and skateboarders must wear helmets.

All living things on a float must be secured.

No open flames.

A hand-hold or other support must be provided for all unit riders who are required to ride in a standing position.

All standing and seated riders must be secured by a safety belt with a quick release mechanism.

Portable generators, compressors or car batteries used on the float must be securely mounted on a vehicle or other substantial base.

All electrical devices must be properly grounded.

Construction materials must be fire/flame resistant or non-combustible.

Generators must have 15/3 AWG (min size) power cords.

All connections must be made with UL approved electrical boxes or devices.

A 5 lb. ABC or a 2A-10BC rated or larger fire extinguisher must be on board. Fire marshal will inspect each unit.

Your unit is responsible not only for your own safety but for the safety of the spectators.

No alcohol, smoking, illegal substances, inebriation.

You must provide a liability release and a hold harmless clause.

Apparel must comply with state laws.

Genitals and nipples must be covered and undergarments must be worn.

Children must be supervised by an adult.

Number of children per adult supervision is five to ten for those children 12 and under.

No child younger than age 6 to 10 walking in the parade, depending on the length of the parade.

Adults must be on floats with children.

Floats must have a skirt.

Only one decorated support vehicle per unit.

The parade committee can grant written approval for any exceptions.

Floats must be made with approved fire retardant materials.

A pickup truck and a trailer will not cut it.

For night parades, all support staff or chaperones walking along the parade route must be dressed in black or in costume.

There will be no movement from truck to trailer.

Flat beds with semi-trucks only.

Semis not allowed.

Middle school students must be on a float.

No children may be left on a float without adult supervision.

Characters whose costumes make it impossible to walk through the entire parade must provide their own vehicle and will not be considered a walking unit.

No riders will be permitted in the back of tow vehicle.

All floats should be at least X feet in length.

Must be in good taste, add to the entertainment value of the unit and not distract from the unit presentation.

Float builder contact information.

Float safety monitor captain name.

All towing vehicles to be fully decorated to match the colors/theme of the float/unit.

All professional floats must have wheel skirts covering the wheels.

Each float must be equipped with a ½" bar and a 1½" eye for hooking a towline in case of breakdown.

Tailpipe for exhaust must extend to side roof or rear, projecting beyond the flat apron.

Signs must appear on the side aprons.
Devices displaying advertisement for any trade mercantile pursuit or business occupation shall not appear above the bed of the float.

Participants will be in period costume.

No political signs, materials, or shirts are allowed on floats or on person participating on the float.

Gasoline must be stored away from any generator.

From the Washington State Autumn Leaf Festival Parade Float Inspection Sheet:
"Driver must have inspection list in his possession on parade day
Driver has 180-degree vision.

Driver has proper ventilation: driver's compartment has been tested and found to be free of carbon monoxide by safety official.

Driver has secondary means of escape.

Float driver has valid drivers license.

Engine is clean of oil and grease residue to prevent overheating and to reduce any fire problems.

No smoking allowed on float.

Brakes, including emergency brake have been inspected and found to be working properly.

Tires have been checked for legal tread depth and adequate tire pressure.

Battery is in good condition.

Float is properly serviced for gasoline, water and oil. No extra gasoline carried on float.

Gasoline tank is of standard auto type.

Float is properly equipped with a UL approved 2A 1OBC fire extinguisher, plus an additional 2A 1OBC extinguisher if a gas generator is used. Must be serviced and tagged and dated within one year.

Towed trailers or floats have safety cables or chains in place and attached to tow unit, towing hooks front and rear are accessible and of sufficient strength for towing float.

All decorative materials used are flame resistive or made by an approved fire retardant.

Exhaust pipes are free of leaks, extends at least 12 inches beyond the float apron. Where pipe is within 12 inches of decorative material, pipe is to be protected by pipe legging.

Each standing float rider must have a wrap around body support or a body support with an approved automotive seat belt. Each seated rider must have a body support or two hand-holds. Seat belts shall be worn on the outside of the user's costume."

Insurance Rules

Have a copy of your insurance available at the parade.

All drivers of vehicles must have personal liability insurance and provide a copy of their proof of insurance with their application.

Owners must provide insurance and proof of liability for animals at the parade and attached to this application.

Failure to provide proof of insurance upon request could result in disqualification.

Name of insured.

Insurance carrier.

"Each commercial parade entry is responsible for the procurement of a minimum of $1 million liability insurance coverage naming (Rockland Festival Corporation) as additionally insured Proof of Insurance must accompany application.

Walkers/Contingent Stewards/Monitors/Outwalkers Rules

Out-walkers are any individuals walking along side of a parade unit.

No monitors required with 1-9 members in group.

2 monitors required with 10-20 in the group.
4 monitors required with 21-40 in the group.

8 monitors required 41-80 in the group.

Must be in costume.

Dress must be uniform with matching t-shirts and or hat with our organization's logo.

Parade walkers must keep up with their parade unit.

Costumed out walkers are highly encouraged so long as they add to the safety of the parade and enhance the theme of the unit and parade. Out walkers cannot slow down the progress of the parade, otherwise they will be asked to leave the parade.

Staging Marshals/Wranglers/Route Marshals

These go by different names. Staging is self-explanatory but wrangler sometimes replaces the staging marshal name. Medium parades are also using route marshals for the parade route itself.

Have the right to accept reject, reclassify, or remove any unit that does not follow the parade rules or the decisions of the parade committeeperson or police.

Will be assigned to each division or unit and will complete the route with that division. They will be clearly marked and their authority must be respected.

Parade Marshals will complete the route with that division or group of entries.

Please provide the name of at least one volunteer from your organization to assist the parade staff with crowd control, driving, traffic control, or organizational duties.

It is the sole responsibility of any entrant to help remove unit(s) that becomes disabled immediately.

Animal Rules

All animals must be currently vaccinated as provided by state law.

No/Yes on Exotic animals.

Pets must be on fixed-length leashes of no more then six feet.

Any obvious animal abuse will be reported...and will result in removal from parade.

No animals will be allowed in the parade without approval by the parade coordinator.

Animals must be on leashes or restraints and handled by someone strong enough to manage them.

Animals must be decorated.

Animal entries must be people and crowd experienced.

Equestrian Rules

Equestrian units must have prior parade experience and verification that the horse is parade safe.

Often have a specific line-up location.

Only one rider per horse.

Horses must be bagged or pooper-scoopers required.

Any horse unit must supply proof of liability in the amount of $1 million.

Lone horse riders not allowed and must be with a group.

Any rider or handler showing inability to control their animal will be removed from the parade.

Rider must own the horse.

Equestrian judging is done on the parade route.

Parade dress for horse riders is required.

Horses must comply with federal and state quarantine regulations. Please contact the USDA.

The California State Horsemen's Association has a pretty good website. There are better ones I'm sure, but for the city slicker parade committees it might be of value.

> "9.1 It is customary to acknowledge the judge(s) and dignitaries on the reviewing stand in the line of march.

Mounted groups carrying flags will maintain the American flag in an upright position. All other flags will be lowered forward to a 45-degree angle while passing the reviewing stand. U.S. Office of Protocol in Washington, DC sets the standards for all flag display, even in parades.

Contestants in mounted groups not carrying flags and matched pair contestants may salute or tip hats in unison. Always maintain contact with the horse when acknowledging the judge/reviewing stand.

Individual contestants may acknowledge the judge with a salute as they pass thorough the reviewing area.

Always maintain contact with the horse when acknowledging the judge / reviewing stand.

Authentic costume class contestants may salute as the custom (culture) dictates.

Always maintain contact with the horse when acknowledging the judge / reviewing stand."

Appendix I Awards

Time and location of awards ceremony.

A unit that has won a prize or an award in the past will not be eligible to win again with that same unit in future parades.

Competition for prizes is open only to non-professional units.

Winners list location.

What will actually be given at the awards ceremony?

When can they pick up their award?

Will they be mailed and if so, when?

Who will receive parade participating plaques?

First ten student organization float entries receive $50!

A plaque to proudly display.

The X highest scores get $X each to be mailed...

$2,000 is paid for each band having at least forty participants either marching and/or playing music continuously throughout the parade. Box lunches are provided for all band members.

When you list your winners, publish the list of Exhibition entries. That way those unit supporters will realize that they weren't being judged and wonder why they didn't win.

Resources

IFEA.com
IFEA World Headquarters
2603 W Eastover Terrace
Boise, ID 83706 USA
208-433-0950
Info@IFEA.com

The International Festivals and Events Association is the premier festival and event association worldwide.

> "With a target audience that includes *all those who produce and support quality celebrations for the benefit of their respective "communities,"* the IFEA's primary focus is identifying and providing access to the professional resources and networks that will, as stated in our mission, *inspire and enable those in our industry to realize their dreams, build community and sustain success through celebration.*
>
> The IFEA exists to serve the needs of our entire industry, all those who share our core values of excellence & quality; *the sharing of experience, knowledge, creativity and best practices; and the importance of "community" building both locally and globally.* Our success lies in the success of those we serve through professional education, programming, products and resources, networking and representation
>
> Behind the scenes of the IFEA is a dedicated, creative and event-experienced staff, ready to help provide the answers, guidance, information, resources, contacts, programming, benefits, and support that you need to be successful."

IFEA Library Resources

> "The IFEA offers the largest catalog of resources, at the deepest discounts, in our industry. The library now includes nearly 100 titles covering almost every topic; as well as selected videotapes, DVD programming, the ENCORE economic evaluation software, and IFEA Webinars On-Demand for those needing to match their own professional educational needs with unpredictable schedules. We are working to build a larger selection of international titles to serve event professionals in every part of the world and to update many of our current,, but still important, IFEA titles. The IFEA Foundation helps to make these resources available and affordable."
>
> Their Bookstore and Resource Center, is a superb source for most any

question you have. Many of the contributors may even be in your state. Check out their website in detail. When you find that their resources fit with what you need, consider joining the association. Their membership rates are below market. Simply make this a parade expense. Students might get in for $75. Attend a yearly national conference and exposition.

Their resources are by the leaders who devote full time to these topics and are experts in their field. Here is an overview of what you will find:

1. 83 books on many of the topics you will want to know
2. 26 $10 International Event magazines with articles on topics as diverse as to what to do when a natural disaster happens in your neighborhood
3. A $10 booklet on Venue Safety and Security
4. Webinars
   - Four on Creativity
   - 18 on Leadership
   - 20 on Economics covering sponsorships and much more
   - 17 on Trends
   - 1 on Time management.

This is just a sampling with new items being added monthly.

IFEA President's Letter

Steven Wood Schmader, CFEE
President & CEO of the International Festivals and Events Association
December 2012

While talking with Eric Fournier, Executive Producer for the Moment Factory, about some of their projects and events, I was reminded of all the moments that surround us every day—some passing without recognition; others touching our lives forever.

And I was reminded of the unique responsibility and opportunities that we, in our industry, have all been given to create those moments for families, friends, individuals and the communities that we serve. But to do that well, we must first recognize and appreciate just what we are talking about impacting. In the tradition of the memorable George Carlin, let's 'take a moment' to realize just what an important role "moments" play in the world around us:

- Whatever it may be, we'll do that task "when we get a moment."
- We "just need a moment to ourselves," preferably a quiet moment, a moment of privacy, even though we know that moments with others can often become our most treasured moments...golden moments, possibly everlasting moments.
- In the course of our day we may experience funny moments, embarrassing moments, scary moments, amazing moments, difficult moments, surprising moments, and even Oprah moments.
- We have our moments of introspection, moments of decision, moments of obligation, moments of truth, and moments of pride.
- We can take a moment to remember, if we are not busy at the moment; but not to worry if we are, because we'll be back in just a moment.
- We have senior moments, aha moments, romantic moments, defining moments, religious moments, eye-opening moments, tender moments, moments of reason, moments of clarity, and oh, crap! moments.
- So as not to risk losing it, we often try to capture the moment.
- We ask if people can't give me just a moment.
- We remember the moment I first saw her/him.
- We reflect upon iconic moments, tragic moments, and great moments in history.
- We tell others that "It wasn't all that great, but it had its moments."
- And most of us have moments we'd like to forget.
- We sometimes get around to things at the last moment.
- We share what happened at that moment.
- We make decisions of great moment.
- And sometimes we are fortunate enough to get our moment in the sun.

By definition a 'moment' is "an important or significant time or occasion; a brief period of excellence or interest"; and that is where our industry comes in, because we all know that in a "moment" anything is possible. All of you, and your peers around the world, every day, are responsible for moments of every imaginable scale and magnitude, usually highly positive. You create, inspire, set the stage for, build upon, make possible and share:

- Olympic moments
- Global moments
- Magical moments
- Disney moments
- Life-changing moments
- Kodak moments (remember those?)
- Family moments
- Festive moments
- Moments of celebration
- Moments of community bonding
- That "one special moment"
- That "one moment in time"
- And best of all, we get to create "unforgettable moments" (until the moment that we top ourselves again). But to do that, we have to clearly recognize what we do and commit ourselves to the levels of quality, creativity and dedication that it takes to produce those special end products, those special moments.

We must identify those partners who care as much about creating those moments as we do and encourage them to join us in building our visions: city officials, sponsors, volunteers, media, suppliers and tourism organizations. Muhtar Kent, the CEO of Coca-Cola, in an interview with CNN last July, was asked why his company sponsors the Olympics and how they quantify the return on their investment. His response stood out to me and I hope to others as well. He replied, and I paraphrase: "I couldn't see a better fusion of our ideals, values and the opportunity to bring communities from all around the world together; that's very much in line with our own values, beliefs and heritage. With regard to return, we can count many things—media mentions, web hits, sales, relationships—but I think it is wrong to quantify everything in the world of marketing, in the world of branding. We must ensure that we still create positive moments and emotions with consumers."

Find those sponsors and protect those relationships. At a time, worldwide, when cities are struggling and decisions are being made to cut budgets at every level, there are cities who recognize the powerful role that events play in protecting and supporting the quality of life in their communities and who, instead of pulling back, are actively revisiting and strengthening their partnerships with those in our industry, assuring that those critically important community events and bonding moments don't disappear. Support those cities and efforts and encourage your own communities to emulate their successes and commitment.

And, just like our sponsors and our cities, please don't mistake the suppliers to our industry as anything less than full and committed partners to your success. If you are truly committing yourself to the quality, creativity and dedication that you will need to create those special "moments," you will need to work with those who are just as committed and passionate as you are. The suppliers and professionals who support the IFEA and our members, every day, have already proven their commitment to our industry. Show your support for them and your event by exploring what they can bring to your table.

My mother passed away ten years ago and I was recently going through some boxes of her personal keepsakes for a family ancestry project that I am working on. As I did so, I was reminded again, as I was when she passed away, of just how many of her photographs, keepsakes and memories with friends and family revolved around events.

In West Virginia, where I grew up, we always attended the Sternwheel Regatta Festival, where the big paddlewheel boats—overflowing with people and music—raced down our river, using the bridges as start and finish lines, and tugboats would engage in shoving contests. We saw John Denver first perform his hit "Country Roads" on the steps of our capital building during a state celebration event. Mom and her friends would go to neighboring Ohio to "Bob Evans Farms" (they own the Bob Evans Restaurant chain, if you are familiar with those), where they would load chickens into giant mailboxes, shoot a cannon to scare them, and see which one flew the farthest (probably not a big favorite of the folks at PETA).

She and her friends went to "Bridge Day" at the New River Gorge Bridge, where once a year they held a celebration and you could walk across the highest bridge in North America. And my parents used to take us in the middle of the night down to watch the circus animals unload from train cars and parade to the venue where they would perform. Those, and many other similar examples, are the things that she remembered, and that we now remember doing with her. Those were "our moments."

And I was recently a part of the Spirit of Boise Balloon Classic—an event that I helped to start twenty-one years ago in our city. On an early morning in the park, as the sun was just coming up over the mountains and the balloons were filling the park and sky with color, I noticed a man in a bathrobe holding the hand of his young daughter, also in her pajamas; the dew had soaked about two inches of their pajama pant legs. I assume they lived nearby and I imagined the little girl making her dad get up to go see the balloons before they launched and flew away, with no time to get dressed and fully ready. I admired his willingness and understanding of the importance to do so. They were sharing a very special moment that neither of them will ever forget.

And the people who create and support those moments— large and small, from around the globe—are those whom we have the pleasure of representing and supporting through the IFEA. Your professional peers, your friends—those whom we look to when we need support and new ideas, motivation and inspiration.

As we start a new year, we are all provided with a whole new set of opportunities to create those special moments—for individuals, for families, for friends, for the communities that we serve. For ourselves, our staffs, our events and our organizations. If you were waiting for it to be clearly identified, this is our moment. Our moment to learn, to build, to imagine, to create, to plan, to share, to help, to provide your own unforgettable, perhaps career- or life-changing moment—or perhaps, to change the world.

I wish you and yours a very happy, healthy and prosperous year. Take time to savor the moment.

"Analytically Estimating Attendance at a Parade"

Attendance figures are a valuable statistical resource utilized to plan, staff, operate, and ensure safe environments for parades. Your ability to estimate possible spectator counts is critical with often limited financial resources for trash containers and restrooms as well as emergency services personnel. Moreover, estimated attendance is considered as a significant quantifier of accomplishment. Fair and honest crowd counts are morally and ethically critical to calculate total marketing impressions as an element of sponsor benefits and total visitors as a multiplier for economic impact reports.

A key control used to when estimating attendance at a parade is to ascertain your possible maximum crowd. This can be a time consuming task, but once completed the data is available for future parades on the same route.

- Begin by calculating the total square footage of available spectator space. Break down the entire viewing area into smaller shapes to compute their square footage and then add the figures for all the areas to arrive at a square footage grand total for the route.

- Next, divide the square footage grand total by a space per spectator figure to determine maximum capacity of the site. Based on research you can squish people standing as a crowd into a minimum space of 1.66 square feet, but this situation is sustainable for only a few minutes so using 4.00 square feet per person is more reasonable. Spectators sitting in chairs, bleachers, or on the ground occupy about 8.50 square feet per person.

For example, in Phoenix we calculated a total viewing area for a 2.5 mile route to be 559,680 square feet with a possibly maximum capacity of 337,157 squished, 139,920 sustainable, or 65,845 sitting spectators without extra items such as coolers or walking space at their rear.

To estimate actual attendance, first visualize a crowd 1 person deep, with standing or sitting spectators occupying a space 2 feet wide. For 1 mile with spectators on both sides you would have 5,260 people. I suggest you mark off each mile on your route into 52 sections of about 100 feet and estimate if the crowd in each section is really this tight and also how many deep. From an elevated position, such as atop a parade float, buildings, or with cameras on balloons a few hundred feet off the ground this task is easier and more accurate. A 100-foot section, tightly packed (50 people wide) and 4 people deep would have about 200 spectators. Add your estimates for each section to determine you final attendance total, which again, is controlled by your previously estimated maximum capacity.

Most importantly, however you decide to accomplish the task, make a plan on how you will estimate attendance in advance, follow through with methodic data collection, and base your final count on the accumulated facts and not a wild, spur of the moment, innumerate guess. Attendance matters and your reputation and that of your organization may also depend on it.

Vern Biaett CFEE
Faculty Associate, School of Community Resources & Development
Arizona State University
(Reprinted with permission, 2012)

ABOUT THE AUTHOR

In the mid 1970s, Ed Tomlinson, a Colorado Realtor by trade, ran the Arvada Harvest Festival Parade for several years. He expanded and turned it over when it became the state's largest parade with 427 entries, including eight marching bands. Arvada, a northwest suburb of Denver, had a population of fifty thousand at the time.

In 1979 he chaired a National Clowns of America Convention. It included a downtown Denver clown parade along 16th Street, which featured some seven hundred clowns and an authentic steam-driven calliope from Kansas.

From 2005 to 2012, he took over the Arvada Harvest Festival Parade once again. It contained approximately one hundred entries, including six marching bands. This popular parade operated without support of a computer and was put together just three months or so beforehand. He retired as parade chair after the 2012 Parade.

In that twenty-five-year time frame Arvada's population doubled to more than one hundred thousand. In the five years he had been parade chair, the parade grew to about three thousand participants, including up to seventeen high school marching bands, with an estimated twenty thousand spectators.

His goal to make it the top community parade between LA and Chicago, by many standards, may have been achieved.

In the late 80's and early 90's he wrote two best-selling books on Colorado real estate taxation. Currently, he is working on a lifestyle book for couples in their twenties and a science fiction treatment (a short version of a screenplay). *Community Parades* won third place in the 2014 Colorado Independent Publishers Association Evvy Book Awards.

Tomlinson is a member of the Colorado Festival and Events Association and the International Festivals and Events Association. In 2014 he was a panelist at their convention. He is a former member of the City of Arvada Festival Commission, a former Arvada Harvest Festival Parade Chair and a Rotarian.

He is very active in the community and has served on many public, private, elected and appointed boards.

If you need help, for a $25 hourly fee, he can be your consultant.

ORDER FORM

Fax orders: 303 922-3062

Email orders: Order@CommunityParades.com

Telephone orders: 303 937-6044

Postal orders: Diamond Publications, 6655 W. Jewell, #218, Lakewood, CO 80232

Please send the following book(s).

$19.95 ___ **Community Parades**
Valuable Tips, Ideas and Procedures on How to Plan, Organize, Produce, Run, Stage or Start an Outstanding Community Parade. Order copies for everyone. Bulk order pricing available.

$4.95 ___ **Your Parade: A Checklist**
As a parade organizer, you know it takes multiple steps to put together a great parade. It also can take years of trial and error before everything falls into place. Use this handy checklist to ensure you are taking all the steps you need for your best parade ever.

$29.95 ___ **The Set:** Includes one copy each of *Community Parades, Your Parade: A Checklist,* plus two *Special Reports* (see below)

$7.95 ___ Special Report: "How to Produce an Award-Winning Community Parade Entry for Just About Free"

$7.95 ___ Special Report: "Get Savvy with the Media: Tips on How to Prepare for a TV Interview and Deal with Reporters

Please print:

Name:____________________________________

Address:__________________________________

City:____________ State____________ Zip_______

Telephone:________________________________

Email Address:____________________________

Sales tax: Please add 7% for products shipped to Colorado addresses.

Thank you for your order.

Please visit
www.CommunityParades.com
to send us your ideas and comments.
Also, check there often for special reports.

—Ed Tomlinson